How Easy Money Selling Your Old Used Books On Amazon!

Earn Money Selling

Used Paperback and Hardcover Books

On The Amazon Marketplace

5th Edition – February 2014

By Steve Johnson

Johnson Publishing Company

Why you need to read this book:

Selling used books on the Amazon Marketplace and on other used book websites is probably the easiest way to earn extra money in your spare time I've ever found. It's low-risk. It's simple to learn. And knowing how to stock up on the books that sell the best will ensure higher profits and quicker sales. That's why this book will make you money. It will tell you what to have on hand before you list your books for sale on Amazon Marketplace and EBay specifically. It will show you how to accurately describe the condition of the used books you find, and it will help you learn how to negotiate the best prices… all so you'll make more money. The return on investment in this simple, easy-to-read guide will more than pay for itself in short order. Plus, you'll find the distilled know-how of a successful Amazon Marketplace bookseller who know is sharing the who, what, when, where and how of online used book selling.

Truly, this is an excellent part-time business for anyone wanting to get rid of their old books to make room in their home or office, or someone who wants to supplement their income with easy, extra cash. No real selling required: just find and stock up on the types of books millions of people are searching for every day, list them correctly and ship promptly.

Enjoy this book. And thank you for purchasing this copy of "How To Make Easy Money Selling Your Old Used Books On Amazon."

Sincerely,

Steve Johnson

Johnson Publishing Company

What You'll Learn Inside:

TABLE OF CONTENTS

CHAPTER 1: How A Fool Idea Turned Into A Part-Time Used Book Business

Yes it's true -- I make easy cash selling dirty old books online. Dirty, used books that I find everywhere -- at garage sales, estate sales, auctions, thrift stores, anywhere I go, there are filthy, unwashed and unwanted books just begging me to pick them up and take them home!

I dust off these unwanted gems, take two minutes to type in a unique 10-digit number, copy-and-paste a pre-written description, set my price and post them online for free, and then I just sit back and wait for the email to show up, saying "Sold, Ship Now!"

The cash is waiting for me. All I need to do is pack and ship the dirty book and bingo! I get paid seconds after I confirm that the books have been shipped. Easy as pie!

Well, there are a FEW things you have to do to make sure you are selling the right dirty books.

Now, this has nothing to do with selling pornography (although old copies of Playboy are big sellers online!). These dirty books are those tomes boxed up from somebody's extra bedroom or attic or barn or garage, and sold for pennies on the dollar to dirty booksellers like me!

You'll want to pick up the dirty books that aren't TOO dirty: torn covers, scribbled notes on text pages, bindings coming unbound. Even dirty book buyers have some standards!

But it's a pretty simple trick to learn how to spot the profitable dirty books all around you... and cash in on this easy way to make extra money in your spare time.

Estate sales and garage sales are an excellent way to get started. When I launched my used bookselling business, I purchased a huge lot of 400 books purchased at an estate sale auction for $87! You'd be surprised how many of those books were clean and nearly new.

But there were plenty of dirty, dusty books in that lot that brought me a pile of pocket change too! You can start for under $500, $100 if you have a large number of books in your own personal collection that you want to get rid of now.

The market for used books is growing every day, but you need to know what books to sell or you'll lose your shirt. I've purchased books to resell for as little as 10 cents a book and effortlessly resold them for upwards of $10 each!

How much can you make? That depends. It depends on the types of books you have for sale. It depends on how diligent you are in finding the top-selling books. It depends on how well you follow through and ship the books on time, protecting your seller rating that is so important for getting future orders.

But, like the title of this e-book says, I think it's very easy to earn $10 a day ($300 a month) to $30 a day ($900 a month) because I do it all the time. More $10 and $20 days than $30 days. But it can be done. Very easily.

And when you've done it, you can pay off bills. Take a vacation you couldn't afford before. Go out to dinner at nice restaurants a few more times a month. Pay off your student loan early. Donate the extra cash to your church or to your favorite charity. It's your money, so you decide how to spend it.

You may find out that you want to reinvest your profits back into your business. This is a good idea because adding more valuable books to your stock will allow you to make higher profits, and you may find new business opportunities as you go about your business of finding and reselling used books.

What's also interesting to note when I review our sales reports is that we are not always the lowest price. Many times a much lower price was available for sale, but we wound up landing the sale anyway.

See, I'm not promising that you'll make $5,000 a week. I won't insult your intelligence that way.

(Of course, if you DO eventually make $5,000 a week, send me some!)

This guide is designed to show you how to spend as little as 1 hour a day operating your own home-based bookstore very cheaply. In fact, the driving force behind the tips and techniques you'll find here in this e-book will be to demonstrate that you don't need to invest in lots of inventory, you don't need to subscribe to expensive services, and you don't need to buy much equipment.

You probably have most of what you need right in your own home (for instance, you likely already had a computer before you bought this e-book, so there's no need to buy another one.) You probably already have a digital camera, you probably already have Internet access, and you probably can pick up shipping supplies for less than $25 the next time you're at Wal-Mart.

I'll show you how I balance do things cheaply and doing things efficiently – and these are not always the same thing. Sometimes, it's true, that you ought to spend a little money to make your task easier.

But we'll get to that later. Right now, I simply want to assure you this:

Anyone can do this. If I can do it, so can you! It's recession-proof. When the economy is slow, it seems like used books just sell all that much better. And, when the economy turns around, I'm sure that these dirty used books will still be sought after ... if you stock up on the best books to sell now and learn how to make money in your spare time doing what I do!

Before We Begin:

Let's cover some of the subjects we'll cover in the pages ahead. These are my own experience, not my opinions. You may not agree with me on everything I write, but you'll know what has worked – and not worked – for me.

We'll discuss:

Hidden and out-in-the-open places where you'll uncover a boatload of books to resell. You'll find where to source all the used books you can sell – right in your hometown. They might be in your own collection, maybe those being tossed out by family, friends or neighbors. I've found books at the recycling center! They are everywhere. You'll find out where to look.

Ways you can guarantee that you'll make a nice profit on almost every book that you purchase for resell online... BEFORE you invest a single penny! Comparing current pricing and sales rank of like books is so easy. You may already have the perfect tool in your pocket right now to do it.

I'll share my own experiences on what to stock up on: the best books that sell promptly, and turn over a nice profit for you. Keep an eagle eye out for these winners everywhere you shop and you can't go wrong. I'll also warn you which books to leave behind. They just take up space.

Related online stores and websites to move merchandise in bulk when it won't sell on Amazon. You'll get bigger sales, move more books all at once, and make your money with this technique.

How I set a strategy for pricing my books for maximum profits. I don't always offer them up for the lowest price – and neither should you. Don't give your profits away. Keep them in YOUR pocket.

Important steps you need to take several times a day (don't worry, it's only 2-3 minutes at a time) so you can keep customers satisfied and coming back for more. Protect your high feedback. Many book buyers judge how well you've served past customers as a major reason for doing or not doing business with you.

Simple trick anyone can do to sell vintage printed products "one page at a time," and make more than selling the whole shebang. But there are things to be aware of.... And I tell you how to steer clear of the problems.

Finally, my opinion on best practices for naming your business, operating your business, and expanding your business... plus, ideas on how to diversify your online revenue in ways that could deliver steady, monthly checks month after month on autopilot.... And you just set it up and practically forget it! Very simple money-making strategy that fits in well with re-purposing used how-to books online.

Ready to begin? Good. Grab a notepad and pen, pour yourself another cup of coffee, and get comfortable in your favorite easy chair. Read this manual all the way through. Make notes as you go along. Write down questions about terms or procedures that seem difficult. You'll absorb what makes sense, and a quick tour of your favorite search engine will guide you to the answers for the rest. In the next chapter, I'll start with a little background that will illustrate how easy it is for anyone – including somebody like me – to get started.

CHAPTER 2: My Background – From Frustrated Online Auctioneer To Happy Bookseller

Back in 2003 I asked my wife Karen if she thought we could make some extra money buying collectibles and antiques at local auctions held regularly through the Ozarks region where we live, and then resell them at a profit on Ebay. I wondered if people who lived in far-flung places across the country, perhaps around the world, would want to buy primitives and antiques that went for a song back then at local auctions.

She liked the idea. I was surprised, because I usually come up with some really dumb ideas. Anyway, we started attending auctions, bidding on things we had no idea about, and loaded up our basement and storage shed with tons of stuff. We were the original hoarders.

I registered for an Ebay username, snapped some photos with my digital camera, posted some listings with photos, and began selling that stuff.

Mostly, because I didn't know what I was doing, I was selling that stuff for too little, or not asking enough to pay for the shipping, or forgetting to do a half-dozen things any idiot would know to do right off the bat. But we stumbled through, made some money, and plowed it right back into buying more stuff. There were narrow walkways in the basement between walls of cardboard boxes packed to the brim with our newfound treasures, just begging to be gone through.

I kept posting. Selling. Packing. Mailing. Scrub, rinse and repeat.

But within a short period of time, we found that sales went flat. The cost to buy, hold and ship the product took up a large percentage of the total sale, and it seemed like Ebay and PayPal were intent on taking a big bite out of the rest.

So, after a couple of years, we scaled back Ebay sales in favor of direct sales through a local antiques and collectibles mall, where we rented a space, prices and set out the junk, and waited for some ~~unsuspecting fool~~ prospective customer, to walk by, spot it, and buy it. We wound up paying $149 a month for the booth, and 11% on everything we sold. Things started off swell, and some months we sold more than $800. But the boom months grew few and far between, and the rent stayed constant as the economy tanked during the Great Recession, so we pulled the plug on that idea.

I figured I'd pack up the merchandise, ramp up Ebay listings, and resume selling online. Still, the junk in the basement and storage shed grew. Once you start going to auctions and garage sales, you never stop. But things were about to change!

Then at one auction in late 2010, an estate was being sold off one memory at a time. Everything that woman owned was now going to the highest bidder. And, one thing that lady really liked was books. Lots of books. Stacks and rows and heaped up piles of books.

The auctioneer approached the task of moving these printed piles of how-to information with predictable aplomb: He sped through the process without much forethought. Gotta move 'em, he reckoned. Started selling so much a stack, and when bidders went dumb and motionless, he offered the books up by the row.

Now these books were stacked 10-15 deep on rows of bleacher pull-out seats. He was selling the books by the row. Highest bid would take the entire row.

I thought these might sell quickly on Ebay. My wife was not impressed with my latest brainstorm. But I forged ahead.

"Who will give me $10 a row?" the auctioneer begged? "$5? 3? Help me out folks. 2?"

At which point, right on cue, I raised my hand. "Two."

He asked for $3, and in the next breath, relented, and said. "Sold. You want them all, right?"

"Yep." I was trying to multiply $2 by 10 rows. Remember, I'm not very smart. I think it was about $20, give or take a few bucks. "Sure. I'll take them all."

Believe it or not, I got nervous. Like I'd made a bad deal, blown my money, made a fool out of myself. That was a BIG pile of books! Now, I had no idea what I had just bought, but I figured that for $20, I was hoping I'd find SOMETHING to sell to cover this amount. Heck, there were hundreds of books here. There had to be 3 or 4 good ones in there.

So that's what I did. We made a trip to the local liquor store to get used boxes, returned to the auction, and started packing up the books.

There were books on religion, dog training, celebrity diets, UFO alien abductions, how-to manuals on all topics, romance novels and Oprah's Book Club editions, vintage magazines, weight loss books and DVDs, religious books, histories and biographies and travel books. Every subject under the sun. They all got packed up, loaded up in my pickup truck and trucked home.

And I had no idea what to do with them.

Karen suggested I try selling the books on Amazon. But I was only familiar with selling on Ebay. I resisted. But then she logged into Amazon and showed me the prices people were getting for used books online at Amazon compared to the ridiculously low prices that books were bringing on Ebay.

I thought, what the heck, what's there to lose? Listing books on Amazon is free. The sign up is free, and only takes about 15 minutes. You can list right away, and if there is a ready buyer seeking out that particular book, you could sell it and make money within minutes.

In fact, later that same night several of the books on the Mormon Church founders and historical biographies sold, covering the entire $20 purchase and then some.

The balance of those hundreds of used, dirty books in my basement were now paid for free and clear. I could sell them cheap and all I'd pay for is the cost of packaging materials and the cost of postage at the U.S. Post Office.

I was hooked.

I got busy posting books. No need to shoot, edit or upload a photo. Amazon's system already has that in place. No need to write a lengthy description. Amazon's system already has the product description ready for your use, with reader comments and ranking information, and pricing research right at your fingertips. It's easy to type in the 10-digit ISBN number and instantly see what new, used and collectible pricing is from other sellers.

It got addicting.

I'd take a stack of books, do a pricing lookup, and be amazed that a book which now cost me zero, was in fact being sold for $6, $10, maybe more than $20.

I started posting books with abandon.

Over time, I added about 1,000 titles to our little Amazon account. It wasn't a true Amazon Store, because I decided not to pay for the optional Seller's Store, which costs at this writing about $40 a month. I could always add that later (but haven't). I could always take advantage of the FBA (Fulfilled By Amazon) program, where they inventory and ship the books for me, but I still haven't done that either.

My goal was to discover how to make money part-time, paying as little as possible, to move the piles of books I had acquired. Add to this the large number of books and magazines we already had and wanted to get rid of, and you can start to understand the excitement I felt when the Amazon "Sold, Ship Now!" emails began pouring into my email inbox!

It's been fun and profitable. Now, I want to share how you can do it too!

See, after learning how to go about finding, listing and selling dirty little books from garage sales, estate auctions, orderly library fundraisers and messy thrift stores, I now know what it takes to make easy money doing this. And now, you hold in your hands my roadmap to making money at home by selling used books online!

What You Need To Do To Make Money In This Business

My advice if that you concentrate on certain books for the highest profit margins. These work for me and they'll work for you too. You make money when you buy, not when you sell. Sometimes it makes sense to pay $2-$3 per book. Not often. But when that book is selling for $25, $50 or more, and selling quickly, you'll make a tidy profit fairly quickly even on a book that you paid $5 for. To get yourself started, only buy books for $1 or less. My average price I'll pay now is between 50 cents and $1.

The following types of printed books, magazines, and other related printed materials sell very well on Amazon… and what doesn't sell on Amazon can be re-sold on Ebay, Etsy or Craigslist websites:

How-To Non-Fiction -- This will be your bread and butter. You'll make more money selling the trade books. Keep a sharp eye of to pick these up. You'll notice them by their size; these measure about 6" x

9" and they usually are 1" - 2" thick. They ship cheaply by USPS standard media mail. The subject matter can be diverse. I've sold books on:

Music theory & music sheet music books

Teacher classroom instruction manuals

UFO Abductions

Ancient Aliens In Egypt

Edgar Cayce books

Astrology

Biographies of celebrities, religious leaders, politicians

Buying and selling commodities

Weight Loss

Cancer Cures

Civil War

Credit Repair

Self-Improvement books

Healing with Herbs

Music sheet music books

CHAPTER 3: Here's What I've Discovered That Makes You The Most Profit In This Business

Vintage Magazines -- Like, Look and Time magazines sported vintage covers, some by celebrated famous artists like Norman Rockwell, and famous photographers. Collectors love to find these. They will pay good money for these. Buy them cheap and you'll make money. The best vintage magazines feature celebrities like Jimi Hendrix or Marilyn Monroe or Albert Einstein of John F. Kennedy on the cover. Better yet, even if the old magazine does not have a pristine cover, don't despair. Clipping out the full-color and even the black and white full page ads inside can be profitable. There are lots of people who like to collect and/or display these in their homes. Framed they make a wonderful piece of folk art. (Note: Because magazines carry advertisements, you cannot legally mail them to buyers using the USPS Media Mail rates, which are wonderfully discounted from the regular First Class Mail or even the Parcel Post rates.) These sell quite well on Ebay too.

Teacher Workbooks and Instruction Manuals -- These are usually sold at very high prices from the original publishing companies. Teachers like to get these online at $8-$15 price range if they can use them in their classroom. They save money. You make money. The kids learn something. Everybody wins. I often find them for cheap and resell for $14.99 to $19.99 each. They move quickly.

College Textbooks -- This is a lucrative, competitive area I honestly have only slightly ventured into, since I seldom come across a good, cheap supply of the latest college textbooks which are in good, re-sellable condition. The few I have picked up are select textbooks that HAVE earned me a huge ROI. Careful you don't get stuck with lousy inventory on these types of books. You might need to get creative and sell as a lot. Plus, I've noticed that a new trend in college textbooks is book rental, not purchase, and I wouldn't be surprised that eventually these textbooks will migrate over to e-books and not even be published in print form. Here is a website which promises to give top dollar for textbooks, plus says they offer free shipping too. I've never tried them out, but here is the website:
http://www.booksintocash.com

Home Schooling -- This can be a profitable line of books. Again, like college textbooks, you want to buy them as cheaply as possible, and the condition has to be used like new, or at least used very good. You'll have very dissatisfied customers in their field if you pawn off shoddy, dirty books to them. You'll suffer a heavy percentage of returns and low feedback scores on your seller profile. Buy these. Just don't buy the dirty ones. Like teachers' classroom resource guides, make sure that the previous owner made copies of practice sheets inside the book. If the forms are filled in with pencil, pen or crayon, leave it alone. Nobody will want it.

Comic Books -- Don't overpay for these. Until you really have a grasp for values, which can be found by reading reference books, going online to check the actual selling prices, and talking with avid comic book collectors willing to share what they know about these comic books. But, if you find a stash of old comic books in a box at a garage sale, and the owner has them marked for $2, grab them. The odds are pretty good you'll sell at least one for $2, and you probably will find a few that will make you money. Just know what you're buying. You don't need to clutter.

Collectible Books -- Amazon limits who gets to list books in its Collectibles listings. You can always resell these on Ebay or on CraigsList, even put out feelers to book collectors. It will take longer to sell these, but sometimes you'll discover a gem like when I bought a vintage book on women's rights from the turn of the 20th century for 25 cents, and it's selling for over $100.

Self-Published & Short-Run Books or Booklets -- These could be good sellers. I've been amazed at doctors and laymen who publish small booklets that have sold really well. Many times these are home remedies or strange health cures which no one would dare publish these days for fear of getting shut down by the FDA or FTC. But these little booklets and manuals often sell for 25 cents or less, and you can resell them for $8-$10 very quickly.

DVDs -- Weight loss DVDs are very popular, lightweight to ship, easy to make money on. Other subjects -- like hypnosis, turkey hunting, dancing lessons -- are also good sellers. DVDs also bundle well on Ebay when sell them as a lot and make a lot more money (example: offer 6 lessons on woodworking for one price, creating a great value for those seeking this type of information). You cannot copy a DVD or an old cassette tape or a video tape. You don't own the copyright. But if you buy the original item at a sale, you CAN resell that item for a profit. You're selling the physical product. If you break the law and steal other people's content, a ton of trouble will drop on you. Don't go there.

Repair Manuals -- Auto repair, appliance repair, home repair. These are big sellers. But some publishers flooded the market over the years with certain types of repair books which sell poorly online (most of these will be listed for 1 cent on Amazon) and aren't worth your time, unless you want to have a doorstop that can also tell you how to fix that door lock when it quits working. vintage automobile manuals, tractor manuals, train set books, antique repair instruction books all have collectors, or maybe hobbyists, who want to know how to fix things. Find these types of books and sell them.

Trade Paperback Books Make The Best Profits

Books – especially the trade paperback books -- are easy to store and economical to ship. What you want to look for is the 6" x 9" non-fiction titles. Stock up on them when you find them in Very Good or Like New condition. They are easy to store. We store our books in a small alcove off one of the upstairs bedroom in our home. It used to be a good place to stack junk. Now the walls are lined with bookshelves full of product. No need to pay for storage or warehousing. The books are pulled, cleaned up, double-checked for accuracy to the listing, wrapped in bubble wrap, inserted into a large manila envelope, addressed, stickered with a confirmation delivery slip, and finally delivered to the post office for mailing.

Afterwards, once we have the shipping confirmation slip, we log back into the Amazon website and enter the confirmation that the books indeed have been shipped, and our commission pops up almost immediately in our account. Confirming the shipment takes only a matter of seconds.

We receive our payments once every two weeks. They are automatically direct deposited into our bank account. They show up like clockwork.

You can sign up as an Amazon bookseller in less than 15 minutes. Their website tutorial takes you by the hand and helps you step-by-step to complete the process.

The next section will demonstrate how easy it is to get signed up and get yourself ready to sell on the Amazon Marketplace.

CHAPTER 4: How To Set Up Your Online Bookstore in 15 minutes or Less

Go to the Amazon Seller page here to review the program and sign-up:

http://www.amazonservices.com/content/sell-on-amazon.htm?ld=AZFSSOA#!how-it-works

Here is the link to the Amazon.com Sellers Guide:

http://g-ecx.images-amazon.com/images/G/01/rainier/help/pdf/Getting_Started_Guide.pdf?pf_rd_m=A2CA1KKALKCX2O&pf_rd_s=top-1&pf_rd_r=1819TR6684CRW8XE3PKK&pf_rd_p=1319579782&pf_rd_t=101&pf_rd_i=soa-how-it-works&ld=AZFSSOAAS

(Stop reading! Go there and download it now. You might want to print it out and follow it step by step. It's a good roadmap to set you along the path to making money online!)

Next, you'll take a little time to help put the right focus on your online selling.

Tips For Setting Up Your Seller Account on Amazon

You might want to take a few moments first, though, and decide on what you're going to name your online bookstore, as well as what your focus will be, as this will help give you direction going forward.

Here's my story:

I decided that because we could concentrate on books, the word "Books" needed to be in there. Very prominently. That's a no brainer. But as we stocked and posted DVD's and CD's and workbook manuals and artists instruction books and recipe cookbooks, I tried to expand the name, only to decide in the end that I'd just add "& More" to "Books" and let it go at that.

Since we operate as Johnson Publishing Company, I just shortened the name: JPC Books & More. That name, thankfully, was available, and it's helped quickly identify us amongst other sellers since we began in this business.

I would suggest that you don't go too narrow in your niche, at first anyway. Often you will find unique books that you never thought of selling, and they will be difficult to sell to your customers if they typically buy woodworking books from you and you introduce a line of pet training books. The two just don't go together.

But I've been able to offer just about every type of pet book, travel book, cookbook, UFO book, crop circle books, books on how to knit an afghan, books on alien abductions, books showing how to play the dulcimer and what to see when you're visiting Texas, every type of celebrity book you can think of, and I'm pretty sure it all comes down to the fact that I added the "& More."

Regarding the types of books to start out with, I'll cover that later. But I'd suggest approaching your book sourcing in a balanced way. Try to select the best books you can find (yes, they can be dirty, but people have to be searching for them before you take those dirty books home! -- I'll show you how you can do this later on.)

The best books means you'll want books that are how-to informational non-fiction, self-help, niched, and pay attention to which books have torn or crumpled covers and loose bindings and, specifically, scads of highlighting and underlining and margin note-taking throughout the inside of the book. It's not that lousy looking books don't sell. They do. But it had better really be in demand. A nice looking book with clean, un-smudged text page edges, and non-creased covers and spines, look really sweet coming out of the shipping envelope and onto the kitchen counter in your customer's home. He or she has paid you good money for this book, and has been anxiously awaiting its arrival for a week, and when they get it, you want them to be amazed it is in much better condition than you described!

I have been stunned how happy some of the customers have been in their feedback, after shipping off a pretty shabby dirty book I found at a thrift store for 25 cents and they paid me $15.00 or more for it, and then they log onto the Amazon sellers website and lavish glowing feedback on how wonderful I am.

So, to keep that all important positive feedback building in my account and staying a 5-star book seller, I now tend to favor buying books that look good over those dirty books I started with (though I still love to pick up those dirty buggers every once in a awhile and make a killing with them!)

Now if you wife would just believe them! ☺

CHAPTER 5: What You Will Need to Get Started As An Online Bookseller on the Amazon Marketplace

You've probably already got some of these items laying about your home. If money is tight, buy small quantities to get started (envelopes, bubble wrap for shipping) to economize. Later on you can buy in bulk and save money.

You will need:

A computer with Internet access – If you're reading this you likely already have a decent one. You'll need it every day for researching book pricing and list books for sale.

Shipping envelopes – Brown manila envelopes sized 8 x 11 and 10 x 13 work really good, although there is an envelope marked a #7, and most trade paperbacks fit snugly into it. I've found these at office supply stores, but you'll need to buy them in boxes of 100 to get the best deal.

USPS Confirmation Delivery slips – These are available free from Post Office. They are the green and white slips that have a peel-and-stick adhesive at one end. Ask for a stack of 50-100 to get started.

Black ink pens – Have plenty on hand for addressing packages, Delivery Confirmation slips, shipping labels and making notes for yourself (Tip: Carry a small notebook around with you and list name and phone number of used book sources you find. For instance, if a local library has a book sale coming up in the Spring, jot down the date, plus the library phone number, to call and make sure the sale hours haven't changed).

Pencils with erasers – Many libraries and some thrift shops will go through the process of marking the inside front cover with a price in pencil before their sale gets started. This price is usually $1, $2, $3 – and you'll need to erase this evidence that you got a terrific steal on this book when you're selling it for $9.99 or more! Erase lightly, and make sure you take your time and don't smear the #23 pencil lead all around. That makes a great book look awful. (Tip: If they find a new place for sourcing books, and you notice that they are marking their prices in ink on the inside or (GASP!) outside front cover, don't buy those books. You might want to talk with the manager and ask them to use pencil on inside, as you resell books. And, I might add, you'll probably may as well talk to the wall, because they probably won't care, and some places will actually feel like you're doing something wrong buying a book for a quarter and reselling it for $10, $25 or more. I don't bother stopping by one large book outlet about 30 minutes from my home simply because the books are all marked this way and the volunteers seem proud of their handiwork. Oh well, it takes all kinds of people to make up a world!

Scissors – For trimming and cutting down cardboard packing protectors for supporting thin booklets or paperbacks. Also, you'll need these to cut up the bubble wrap you may use to protect books during shipment (I do, and it's a great way to custom-fit a snug wrapping around the book and protect it during transit ... plus, you'll save money over buying padded shipping envelopes as you get started).

Bubble wrap – You can buy a small roll of clear bubble wrap these days at Wal-Mart for about $4 to get started. This will save you money vs. buying bubble wrap envelopes and help you ship items they you might wind up selling on Ebay or on other online sellers websites.

File folders – Use up some old manila file folders you were going to get rid of if you don't want to buy new ones, which cost about $5 for a small package. You can cut these into two pieces, one to protect front of book and one to protect back cover of book, once you slide the book into the shipping envelope.

Clear heavy-duty shipping tape & tape gun – You'll need the tape gun and 2-3 rolls of clear tape to get started. You can buy the smaller plastic tape dispensers for about $3 each if you're short on cash.

I like the heavier tape gun. They seem to last forever, easy to work with too.

Cleaning supplies – You probably already have these in your kitchen: paper towels, small clean brush, and warm water. Don't use cleaning sprays to remove stains from books or the dust covers. Most times you can put a small amount of warm water on a paper towel, swipe it across the glossy dust covers, and put a clean shine to the book. Don't use cellophane tape to fix tears in the spine or book cover; just describe them in your listing, and mark condition as Used – Acceptable if you consider that the book as a whole deserves to be sold in this condition. Stand over a trash can and use your dust brush to sweep any cobwebs, spider eggs or loose dirt from the top, side edge and bottom of the book to make that dirty book look presentable. Again, if there are dirty or water stains long the outer edge of the text pages, then make sure you add this to your description listing. People will buy these books, but they are doing so for the information inside; it's best to warn everyone that they should be expecting a bit of a mess when they open up your envelope!)

Bookshelves – Needless to say, this business inventory tends to take up lots of room, so set aside a spare bedroom or a cool, dry place in your home that has low humidity, away from windows that sweat to prevent damage to the paper in the books, and invest in or build some shelving to hold your books. Arrange them in a way that makes sense to you, whether you group them alphabetically or in small stacks of similar subject matter. Good bookshelves help speed up your pulling-and-packing time after books have been ordered, it's late at night, and you're stumbling around needed to find that book which needs to be in the mail the next day. Plan to spend a minimum of about $30-$50 for a bookshelf that will hold 200 paperback books.

Work Table – Yes, you can use your dining room table, but having a designated work table like a long folding table that can be stowed away in a utility closet is a nice way to get an assembly line going for (a) listing books and (2) packing books for shipment. I found 3 six-foot folding tables once at OfficeMax on sale for $15 each. I keep one handy to go to work in basement cleaning, listing and prepping books to go into my inventory which is kept in a small alcove off a bedroom upstairs in my home. We lined the wall using white pine boards and wall shelving strips and brackets on one side, and 4 bookshelves on the other side. In all, I can sift through the 1,000+ books stored up there and get my hands on any particular book I need to ship within 1-2 minutes.

Mobile Smartphone – OK, this is optional, but quite advantageous. Most cell phone smartphones will take a big chunk out of your monthly budget. Mine seems to run about $100 a month. But why not consider it an investment for staying plugged into the world around you. I was late to the party upgrading to a smartphone. I resisted for years even getting a basic cell phone. But I finally upgraded to the Motorola DroidX in 2011. Now I couldn't live without my smartphone. I have access with my data plan to check pricing at Amazon while I'm browsing books at a thrift store on a Saturday afternoon. If I spot an item at an auction that I think might resell well on Ebay I can log online and do a search of like items. That way, I know ahead of time if I'm right or wrong. No guess anymore. I get email sales alerts right on my phone. I can access my website anywhere, anytime. If I have a question I can go to a search engine, type in keywords, and find what I need. There is a lot of free information available. There are plenty of free apps online now to help you build a business. Stay away from the free games, and maybe you'll get something done each day! Plus, there are a host of book scanners and PDA's with service plans that can help you scout out books to sell. We'll note some of the most popular ones later on.

Account Set-Up -- You will need a business checking account. Your earnings from your book sales are direct deposited into your account. Ask for a free debit card to go with account, and you won't need to write many checks out of this account. You can use the debit card to make the purchases you'll need to start and operate your bookselling business. Other needs are:

You will need a credit card -- to confirm your sellers account the day you get started (it doesn't get charged again after that).

You will need a phone number – home number or cell phone number – that Amazon will use to send you a confirmation call or text message to confirm your identity when setting up account (this phone number doesn't get published on your online storefront unless you want to put it there – and I'd recommend against that. Your customers need to contact you via email anyway).

You will need a valid email address -- to send messages and receive book sale notifications and to check email notices regarding returns. I'd recommend getting a new Gmail account, and keep your business and your private email accounts separate.

Of course, you'll find your own "needed things" that will help you ramp up your bookselling business. Probably the best thing you also will need is a scheduler – whether it's the free schedule you can download at http://www.findhow2.com/sell-on-amazon/index.html of one of your own choosing – so you can start the habit of good time management.

Calculate how many hours a week you want to devote to this business. A good start for you might be 1 hour a day; 30 minutes in the morning, 30 minutes at night. As your sales grow, the time you spend working listings and fulfilling orders will grow, too. Figure out in advance with a daily/weekly/monthly schedule how you'll cope with the changes.

Perhaps you'll need to wake up 30 minutes earlier, perhaps you'll need to spend 30 minutes during your lunch break to run parcels to the U.S. Post Office in your town. Whatever it takes, by planning ahead for it, you'll be that much farther ahead when sales DO spike for you.

Here is a photo of our storage area in an upstairs alcove. I get my exercise running up and down the stairs shelving and retrieving books!

This area of our house was going unused, and it serves as an out-of-the-way storage space to house over 1,000 books in our inventory. As you can see, having just 1,000 books can be a problem if you aren't prepared. Plus, since I'm terrible at organizing the books in easy-to-retrieve order that makes sense for anybody else, I could benefit myself from a long afternoon reshuffling the books to make them easier to find. The procrastinator in me has agreed to start on that project... tomorrow.

And here is a photo of some outgoing books, showing how I wrap up the books in bubble wrap then slide them into the regular mailing envelopes, and topping off the package with free USPS Delivery Confirmation green-and-white slip to help make sure the customer (and myself!) can track the package as it crawls through the U.S. Mail to its final destination. Proof that you can even do this business on a kitchen counter!

(Note: you no longer need to use the green and white Delivery Confirmation slips on your book shipments. The USPS Tracking Number is printed right on your postage receipt).

To sum up this chapter, here's an article I published on EzineArticles back in early 2012 which still contains some helpful advice today:

"Get Started Selling On Amazon Marketplace: Rookie Mistakes To Avoid"

By Steve Johnson

Mistakes happen. They are a part of life. But mistakes are no way to build your used book business, selling used books, music CDs and instructional DVDs on the Amazon Marketplace. Here are six 'Rookie Mistakes' I made that you should avoid if you want to have a long-term successful business selling on Amazon:

Mistake #1: Thinking the customer wanted a thank you note. My initial idea was to build a relationship with people who purchased from me, drive them back to my Amazon Bookstore page, and sell more books to a happy customer. But the customer belongs to Amazon, not me. Adding a 'Thank You' note is permissible under Amazon's Terms Of Service (TOS).... but it doesn't really help you make any money.

Bottom line profits suffer. You have to pay the cost of the card, the time it takes you to fill it out, and additional postage you will be charged, as you must pay the letter's first class postage on top of the USPS Media Mail rate when you put anything inside the package containing your shipped books.

Doing all this work is unproductive. The customer is not looking for a new place to shop. They are looking for certain titles to buy. If you have what they are looking for, then they'll be back. The best way to have an old customer purchase from you again is to source those similar types of books, list them at a competitive price in the Amazon Marketplace, and wait.

Mistake #2: Forgetting that book descriptions are all buyers have to go on. The majority of the problems I've had selling used books on Amazon were my own fault. Early on, I was not careful making sure that the book I was listing was free of highlighter markings or scribbles in the margins. This is what most buyers want to know, since they cannot pick up the book and thumb through it, they depend on the seller to accurately and honestly describe the book for them.

I remember one time listing such a marked-up book as "Like New" because I was in too big of a hurry to actually thumb through the inside text pages. The cover looked like new, the spine was not creased. But when the customer received the book and found it marked up, he was incensed.

I immediately refunded the purchase price, the original shipping and the return shipping plus 10% premium for taking up the buyer's time having him make a trip back to the Post Office to return the book.

But I learned to be extra careful describing my books. I usually take longer to list books now -- sometimes three times as long -- as I flip through pages of the book, looking for markings or new edition indicators. And I now list books I once described "Like New" as "Used - Very Good." This change has helped eliminate any complaints about the condition of the books I've sold over the past year.

Mistake #3: Not being careful with labeling packages for shipment. I'm a pretty good speller. My handwriting is good. But I do get in a hurry. There always seems to be distractions when I'm addressing book packages to take them to the Post Office. I have more than one time put the wrong buyer's address on the wrong package.

Numbers can get transposed if you're not careful, and zip codes could get mixed up. Take your time and double check shipping addresses, city names and zip codes before heading off to the Post Office. You'll save yourself a lot of aggravation later on by doing so.

Mistake #4: Not organizing book inventory correctly. One mistake I keep making comes down to my own need to get organized better. By this I mean that sourcing, buying and listing the books is easy for me; getting them sorted and organized so I can quickly find them again when the orders roll in is not so easy for me.

It seems I have an innate need to relive the frustration of hunting down books for 20-30 minutes when the orders come in, muttering such things as, "I know I saw that book in this stack... no, this stack... no, this stack." Books that are too hard to locate and retrieve quickly will squander your valuable time, and that reduces your profits when you could be doing something more productive... like listing more books.

The solution: group your books by subject, then figure out a simple way to organize them that makes sense to you -- by date listed, by author's last name, alphabetical by title -- whatever system works for you, pick one and stick to it. And to store your books, you need to set aside one room in your home with easy access, making sure it is dry and not too humid, not too close to windows which let in damaging sun rays, and a sturdy lock on the door if you have small children or grandchildren packing crayons.

Mistake #5: Spending too much money on shipping supplies and postage. My initial shipments went in expense padded envelopes I picked up at a local discount store. I paid too much and lost a lot of profit in those early days.

Now, I buy the larger manila envelopes, and I reinforce the seams and the corners with clear plastic shipping tape and I wrap the books in bubble wrap. The wrap keeps the books snug and secure in the mail (protecting their condition without adding much weight to the package), the clear shipping tape keeps the envelopes from bursting open during transit, and I have never had a complaint with the way the books arrive. Along the way, I am sure I've saved at least 30 percent on shipping supplies.

As far as postage, initially I planned on offering First Class Package rates to deliver the books faster. But the cost is close to 50 percent higher than Standard Media Mail, and the customers seem to understand that they are not paying for expedited shipping. There have been no complaints using Media Mail from the folks who have purchased used books from me on Amazon.

Mistake #6: Forgetting to use vacation settings at the right time. When I travel out of town, and I cannot fulfill orders, I always log onto my Amazon Seller Account homepage the day before I leave, click on the Store Settings, and select the vacation settings. This immediately removes my inventory from the Amazon system, and although I don't make any sales on that day, I can concentrate on packing and getting ready for my trip.

When I return, I don't click the 'Active' button in my account until the airplane has safely touched down at my home airport.

One time I made the mistake of resuming listings the day before I was to return home, but my flight got delayed due to bad weather and orders came in while

I was stuck in the Dallas-Fort Worth Airport. Fortunately, because you have two business days to ship the books, I had some wiggle room and I was able to beat the deadline once I did arrive home.

These six mistakes were not the only ones I've made along the way, but they helped teach me how to better manage my time and resources so I could make more money and satisfy more customers. I made the decision to turn these mistakes into learning opportunities to help me build a better, more profitable used book business. I hope they can help you do the same, because the only real mistake you can make is in not starting your own part-time used book business to earn extra income. As basketball great Michael Jordan once said: "I can accept failure, everyone fails at something. But I can't accept not trying."

The next section is my personal guide for finding the best inventory of used books and previously owned DVDs and CDs that will make you money.

CHAPTER 6: How To Buy Books Literally For Pennies On The Dollar and Resell Them Online For Huge Profits!

I can't count the number of times I've bought a book that originally sold in a regular bookstore (anyone remember those?) for $24.95 plus sales tax, and I paid 50 cents, then turned around and resold it for $10, $20, maybe even more than $30 online. I have gotten free books from workshops and classes and from people wanting to get rid of books, that once sold for top dollar; I posted them online, and eventually, many of them sold off to the tune of $10, 20, sometimes more than $50!

Here's an example of a hardcover book that I bought for 50 cents, and it sold within one week for $24.99, plus $3.99 for shipping and handling. After Amazon took its cut of $6, I was left with almost $23. After the $4 cost of packing and mailing the book, and then deducting the cost of the 50 cent book, I had a net profit of $18.50 – almost 4,000% profit!

Here's another example of a mass market paperback called "The Bad Ones." It was in pretty rough shape when I discovered it in a local thrift store. Would you pay 50 cents like I did for this book?

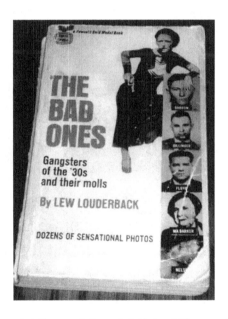

I hope you would have! I sold this 50 cent paperback for $9.99 and it was only listed for sale for about one week!

Finally, here's another paperback. This is a vintage book that I picked up with a large lot purchase. Since several of the books that sold within the first month more than paid for the entire inventory I came home with, this one was left over, free and clear. So my cost was zero. Would you have bought this one for a dime? For 50 cents? A $1 bill?

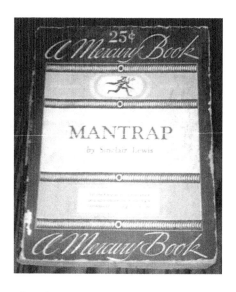

I hope you don't plan on paying more than $1 on books like this. This one sold for $6.95. After packaging, shipping and deducting for Amazon's seller fees, I made a little over $3 on this paperback…. So if you paid more than $1, your time spent on listing this book, packing it up and running to the post office was, at best, a break even sale. Since I had this one already paid for, then the whole $3 was mine.

I could go on and on about the incredible finds. It happens all the time in this business. These books look pretty roughed up to my eye, but they are wanted by avid readers and researchers. And that's not even considering that some people really focus in on the rare, collectible books online.

Personally, I don't seek out "collectible" books. Indeed, I have found some rare books and have earned a nice profit from them; but since Amazon restricts who it allows to list books in the "Collectible" category, I usually avoid adding these to my inventory when I'm out and about sourcing books for resell online.

Ways to negotiate best pricing

I like to buy my books in lots. You get the best deal this way. If you are buying from some thrift stores staffed by volunteers, good luck negotiating better prices. Save your breath. The management of these places usually forbids haggling and making deals. I think it's because they don't want to slow down the cash register clerk from her duties, chasing down the manager to see if they'll knock 50 cents off the price of a hardcover book.

But what you can do is speak directly to the manager and offer to take a box of 50-100 books off their hands for 75 cents a book. Those books might take months to move the way they're doing it now. You never know. The worst that can happen is they'll say 'No.' They won't scratch your eyes out or bite you. At least they shouldn't.

I wouldn't pick the books, lug them up to the check-out counter, and then start negotiating. I'd do it first, before I selected the books I wanted. If they say no, then I'd probably leave. You might want to browse through the book bins and shelves to seek treasure. I'd be off to the next place where I could negotiate finding lots of books in a short period of time, getting them home, and getting them listed online.

Like I said earlier, my best deals have been at auctions, where I've bought literally a truckload of books for pennies a book. Yes, a lot of them were stinkers. I boxed those up in about 20 boxes, and donated them to an animal shelter thrift shop in our hometown. I got a tax deduction receipt that gave me a $300 tax deduction on my federal income taxes. If you're in the 15% tax bracket, that would give you a $45 deduction; if you're in the 28% tax bracket, that would slice $84 off your tax bill. Much better than hauling them to the landfill.

Find your own best approach when negotiating, whether it's at an estate sale auction or a garage sale. I've found that on the final day of a garage sale, the owners are primed to start giving away the stuff. They don't want to haul it back into their garage or into their basement. They want it gone. It's not a bad idea to show up late Saturday morning after the rush is over from a 3-day garage sale and the owners are relieved their ordeal is nearly over.

It's important to count the number of books, and find 4-5 good sellers you know would pay for all of them and leave you a profit left over.

Perhaps the conversation could go like this:

YOU: Hi, had a good sale?

THEM: Yes, we've been swamped. Just about ready to shut 'er down.

YOU: I see you've got a lot of books left over. How much are you asking?

THEM: They're marked $2 each, but we're willing to deal.

YOU: OK. (Pause) I could take them off your hands and save you from having to drag them back inside. I never can get too many books. How about…. $15 bucks for all of them?

THEM: Oh I don't know. Let me ask my husband… No, we could go $1 each.

(At this point, frown, act disappointed, don't say anything. Look at the books lovingly. Like you're saying goodbye to a dear friend. Look them in the eye and say)

YOU: I could do $20 for the whole box, that's the best I could do today.

(Don't say another word. Just stand there. 9 times out of 10, hubby won't want to lug the books back inside. He's anxious to grab the $20 bucks you are holding out in your hand and let YOU lug the books to your car.)

With practice, you'll be bringing LOTS of book lots home every weekend with this technique.

You might also want to let people know you collect books on certain subjects.

I've emailed owners of large book collections when they advertise on Craigslist.org and I've never been able to land good deals. The people I've dealt with …. Tried to deal with anyway …. Put so much stock into their books, they want to sell them for practically what it costs you to buy them used on Amazon in the first place!

Needless to say, I don't often source books online from Craigslist… though that website is a great place to get rid of lots of unwanted books cheaply!

Another thing to watch out for is when you arrive at a yard sale, garage sale, estate auction, whatever sale you're going to, and you see a print out of items being sold online at Ebay or even at Amazon, and they've underlined the selling price. And their selling price is right in line with that printed out price.

My advice: walk away.

They believe they have treasure. They won't sell it cheap. Suggest that they put it on Ebay to get that price. And, if you have time, stop in at the end of their sale and offer pennies on the dollar, tell them you'd really like to round off your collection of this author's book (no need to complete the sentence, "So I can resell it and make money" ... they don't need to know that!) and offer to take it off their hands. Most times you'll be wasting your time. Some people are what I'd term "professional junkers" – they work 2 or 3 days trying to hawk items that ought to be carried straight to the dump, hoping that somebody will come by and be dumber than they were for buying the knick-knack in the first place, and give them enough to soothe their conscience.

Don't be like that. Be in a hurry. You want to cover the most sales in one day. Wasting time going back around is a waste of money. Of course you could always get their phone number and call them before they do haul their treasures to the trash.

Library book sales can be a goldmine…. sometimes

You can find popular annual or semi-annual book sale fundraisers at most public libraries. These often feature great deals on books that patrons have donated. Usually, they are in Like New condition and have never even been cracked open. Non-fiction trade paperbacks like these often go for 25 cents to $1 each, and you can make a lot of money… especially on the final day when most libraries offer a "Bag Sale" offer.

I went to one last year. They handed out these large brown paper grocery bags to everyone, and it was $3 a bag. I didn't even know they made those bags anymore.

Do you know how many books you can fit into those large brown bags?

Believe me… you can fit a LOT in there!

I bought 2 bags, paid only $6, and when I got home, counted them out and determined I'd paid about 10 cents each. One of the books sold within the next 2 weeks for far more than the $6 so the rest were free and clear. Many of those books sold quickly. Some, not so quickly. Some will never sell. I plan to cull those, give some to friends, perhaps re-donate to that same library and let them make money on them all over again. I got my money out of those books.

Maybe it's time they went back to work to make the library even more money, eh?

You can find updated state-by-state lists of library books on the Internet. My favorite is http://www.booksalefinder.com

Like I said before, you will become a good negotiator with practice. Once you become confident in how much books are selling for, you'll know how much you can afford to spend on them. And when you know how much you can spend, and make it a habit never to pay a penny more than that, the people you negotiate with will begin to feel that you are serious and confident, and they'll likely trade the books they want to unload for a lot less than they were originally asking for them.

All you have to do is ask!

Next, we'll explore how the money from used book sales at Amazon gets broken down, and how you make money on the books you're stocking up on.

CHAPTER 7: Breakdown on How Amazon Deducts Its Commission and Fees From the Books You Sell on Their Website

Amazon is pretty straightforward in how it operates – and makes money – off their program. When I first started, I was concerned that their fees and various charges they deducted from third-party book sales seemed to be pretty excessive. However, as I reasoned it through and with more than two years of successful online bookselling behind me, I now understand that the immense traffic flowing through Amazon.com is worth the price of admission.

No, you don't get to send along personalized envelope stuffers or re-contact the customers later with special offers. They are NOT your customers; they are AMAZON's customers. If you don't like that, then don't play in their multi-billion dollar playground! I'm not saying this to be rude. It's just the way it is.

Amazon branded itself as THE place to go find books. People who are looking for used books – whether to locate an out-of-print edition or to save money by not shelling out for new prices – pay Amazon for the book. When you deliver Amazon pays you a portion of what they paid. They keep the rest. I think I figured once that I got to keep 60-65% of the average sale. The secret, bottom-line, is that if you buy right, keep your overhead next to zero, and do the work yourself, you can make $5, $10, $25 a day and sometimes a whole lot more, by selling good used books online!

So let's review the most recent Amazon chart of fees and charges so you'll know what to expect:

Referral Fees Charged to Seller (On Sales Price):

Books	15%
Music	15%
Video & DVDs	15%
Software & Computer Games	15%
Video Games	15%

Book sells for $10. The referral fee is 15%, $1.50.

Book sells for $20. The referral fee is 15%, $3.00

And so on.

Add to this a flat variable fee on every order:

Variable Closing Fees Charged to Seller (Per Item):

Books	$ 1.35
Music	$ 1.35
Video & DVDs	$ 1.35
Software & Computer Games	$1.35
Video Games	$1.35

Finally, there is a flat $ .99 charge for each sale unless you are subscribing to an Amazon Webstore; under those rules you pay $39.99 a month at the time of this writing to have the service, and those $ .99 charges are waived. This is ideal once your sales consistently pass 40 sales a month (10 a week). Until then, pay the 99 cents. You'll know when you can afford the extra $39.99 charge to grow your business.

Every book you list for sale on Amazon waits on the virtual online shelf until it sells... or you take it out of inventory. You can list 99% of the books published today (some publishers restrict their titles from third-party sellers on Amazon; I don't know why but they do).

Best of all, you can list it for free. No charge. List one book or 1,000 books. No charge, and it stays there on the virtual bookshelf until it sells. This is a nice departure from the way Ebay operates, where you're charged to put items up for auction or sale, whether it sells or not, requiring relisting and relist fees every 7-10 days. Needless to say, this is one of my favorite reasons I like to sell on Amazon! List it once and you're done!

When the book, DVD, comic book, whatever you're selling, actually sells and the buyer is charged, you'll receive an email alert that reads "Sold, Ship Now!"

and it will list the title of the book and all the details of the sale.

Most importantly, you will get a breakdown of your net revenue. Out of that amount, you'll need to pay for the product you're selling, pay for the shipping envelope, and pay for the postage to get it mailed to the buyer, and still have something left over for yourself in the way of profits.

If you're not making money, you're not going to be selling books -- dirty books or clean books -- on Amazon or anyplace online for long. Eventually you'll go broke, they'll auction off everything you own, and somebody like me will come in and scarf up all the books you collected. So be careful there.

So How Much Can You Make Selling Books On Amazon?

Here's how to breakdown for Amazon's commission on your sale works out for a book that you list and sell for $9.99.

$9.99 Sale price of the item

$3.99 Shipping credit

-$1.50 Referral Fee of 15% of the sales price of book (note: fee varies if you're selling other items. See referral fee chart on previous page.)

-$1.35 Variable Closing Fee

-$0.99 Fixed Closing Fee (waived for Pro Merchant Subscribers)

=$10.14 Total deposited to your seller's account

"Woo-Hoo!" you're shouting! "I made over $10 bucks."

Nope. Hold on Charlie. Now you've got to pay for:

The price of the book (hopefully no more than 50 cents when you shop smart)

The price of the shipping envelope, bubble wrap, padding, cardboard and packaging tape.

The price of USPS standard media mail postage (this is the most economical way to ship books. If you're shipping other items -- even magazines -- this rate will not be available to you, and your postage could cost you twice as much as media mail. Learn the rates. See media mail chart below listed in this e-book for most current rates.)

Sooooo -- Deducting the price of the book you are reselling (50 cents) from the average shipping/packing costs ($4.00) you will pocket a profit of $5.64.

Not much. But sell 5 books on the average day and you will profit nearly $30 a day – 30 days of that and you're making an extra $900 a month! Not bad!

But if you overpay for the book -- say $5 -- added to the shipping and packing costs, you would only net 64 cents!

This is important. Remember: Never overpay for a book. Only pay $5 for book if it is a quick seller on Amazon (within the top 50,000 of book sales) and it is reselling for a multiple or 4-5 or more. (Example: your $5 book is selling quickly for $24.99. In this instance, you can make money buying books like this. But, again, buy smart. You don't want to stock up on a bunch of $5 books that you wind up selling for 25 cents at a garage sale down the road!

Summing up: Aim to buy your books at 50 cents each and list them for sale at $7.99 to $19.99 each. Sales you make at the lower end will cover your costs and you'll make money on quantity of sales; sale you make at the higher end will be nice scores that you can crow about and be glad you bought this e-book from me!

CHAPTER 8: How to Save Money on Postage & Shipping Supplies When You Ship Orders

Never overpay for shipping.... but DO pay for one thing at the post office and you'll make your seller ratings soar!

Always use the USPS Standard Media Mail – it's the cheapest way to send books. Pack your books tightly and use protective packaging (bubble wrap or even manila file folders work well here). Don't use white large envelopes as they show through the contents of the package, and some buyers will prefer privacy.

I always use the USPS Tracking (previously called "Delivery Confirmation") option. As of this writing it adds a full $1.05 to the shipping cost to a Media Mail shipment, but I feel there are five reasons it's worth it:

Both you and the buyer can track the shipment enroute

It gives the buyer confidence that the book will arrive safely

It gives confirmation to Amazon that you have, in fact, shipped the book on time

It protects you from unscrupulous buyers who claim they never received the book (a rare occurrence, for sure, but this practically eliminates any chance of this happening!)

By offering this as a free service, you are setting yourself far apart and above other booksellers who are 'penny wise and pound foolish.' You're giving something free that appears to be a great value to your customer, and at the same time you are protecting both your inventory and your all-important sellers' rating (more on that later)

(Update: Lately, I've found the USPS workers are asking if I want to add tracking, and are only too happy to charge me the regular $1.05 per package. However, when I declined recently on a non-Amazon order that needed to be shipped, they added the USPS Tracking label anyway. I objected, saying I didn't want to pay for it. They didn't charge me, and the tracking number showed up on my receipt anyway. So, for the time being, I'm just saying 'No' when they ask, and I'm getting this confirmation for the the buyer. If and when this changes I'll update this book. For now, keep the extra money in your pocket.)

Remember that you'll still need to confirm shipment to get paid. And, if you can't produce proof that you shipped the item in the event of a dispute, Amazon will side with the buyer, and you won't get paid. I warned you!

Now, several readers have pointed out that this business is all about watching the margins, and that there is a more economical way to buy tracking services: purchase your USPS postage online through the Amazon Sellers checkout system. You'll need to invest in a small postage scale (the one at my local post office is selling for $39.99), and you'll need to learn how to purchase postage online.

I'll admit that I'm quite lazy. I live in a small town, and it's easier for me to drop in the post office during the lunch hours, have the postal clerk weight the packages, and pay using my credit card. I'm usually in and out of the post office in less than 10 minutes.

But I do agree with them that you need to get wise about watching your margins in this business, and finding each and every way to maximize your net profits.

Wholesale sources for book shipping supplies

You'll make more money by buying these necessities right. Starting out, buy only what you need. But when you get to the point where you are going through 100 envelopes a week, it's time to start shopping for better pricing and make more money.

Sometimes I'll find super bargains at a local Staples or Office Max. I recently bought a box of 100 qty 9" x 12" manila envelopes for $7.99. By reinforcing the edges with clear packing tape, and inserting trimmed pieces of old file folders to protect the books, I've been able to ship cheaper without sacrificing mailing package protection.

I like this place for its product line too. Wide selection, decent pricing: www.uline.com

The USPS Media Mail chart is list below:

Media Mail Rates (updated Feb. 2014)

Weight Not Over (lbs)	Single Piece
1	2.69
2	3.17
3	3.65
4	4.13
5	4.61
6	5.09
7	5.57
8	6.03
9	6.49
10	6.95
11	7.41
12	7.87
13	8.33
14	8.79
15	9.25
16	9.71
17	10.17
18	10.63
19	11.09

20	11.55
21	12.01
22	12.47
23	12.93
24	13.39
25	13.85
26	14.31
27	14.77
28	15.23
29	15.69
30	16.15

Although not required as of this book update, the USPS Tracking service is a valuable way to stand out from the crowd of Amazon Third-Party Sellers by adding additional service to your customers.

You won't find a better deal on sending a used book than media mail! Keep the package light; if it's less than one pound, the single piece cost is $2.69 plus the current charge for Tracking by the USPS (very much recommended as you're starting out and building your reputation, credibility and feedback score).

You CANNOT insert flyers and thank you notes inside the media mail envelope. You can, but you'll pay an extra 49 cents for the cost of a First Class stamp. I don't bother. Remember, the customer is not YOUR customer; it is AMAZON's customer, so you're not going to be re-selling them anything. You are allowed to insert a thank you note with your outgoing shipments. But I quit doing that one month after I started. It didn't seem to help getting people to return to shop my online store. People are searching for specific BOOKS.... Not at specific OUTLETS. They don't care where the book is coming from. They just want the best deal, and they want it as quickly as possible. By using media mail you'll be sending your book the slowest way, but I've never gotten any negative feedback by sending ALL my fulfilled orders this method.

Do you really need to buy a postal scale for this business?

I personally don't use a postal scale to pre-weigh my book shipments. I figure it's a waste of time and money, because I'm going to ship USPS media mail, and the rate is the rate. If I'm selling a typical 6" x 9" trade paperback, my shipping cost and fee for delivery confirmation (tracking the delivery to final buyer) ranges from $3.50 to $4.00. You can drop the delivery confirmation and save $1.05 off these rates (whenever the USPS decides to start charging for this again) but then, you wouldn't have any way to prove the book was delivered, and you are taking away a unique selling proposition that can help you land more sales.

I'm convinced that because my book listings prominently feature the fact that we offer free delivery confirmation on all sales "to ensure accurate, timely delivery to you," that helps us land sales other Amazon sellers aren't getting. People are naturally skeptical sellers will follow through. Maybe they've been burned before. By offering this extra for no extra charge, our customers have a way to track their orders and they get the warm fuzzy feeling that they won't get scammed. Win-win, baby!

However.... If you already or you soon plan to sell collectibles or heavy items on Ebay, purchasing a postal scale to calculate shipping weight is essential, as this will help you determine an accurate amount that you should charge for shipping when you submit your auction or buy-it-now listings.

Don't pay too much. You don't want to cut into your profits any more than you have to in this business!

But Amazon actually has a program where they handle all the shipping for you.... And we'll cover that next!

CHAPTER 9: Is the Amazon FBA Program Worth All The Extra Trouble and Expense?

Selling used books from home doesn't mean you always have to fulfill your book orders from home. You can leverage your time by taking advantage of the Amazon FBA Program. FBA stands for "Fulfilled By Amazon," and, as the program promises, your books are warehoused and shipped from an Amazon Warehouse when somebody places an order and they choose your book. All you need do is find the books, list the books, ship the books to Amazon, and they'll take care of the rest.

Here is a breakdown of how the FBA Program works. You can check for updates on the program at Amazon.com

(Compare the FBA program here)

There are pros and cons to the FBA program (My opinion):

Pros -- You reach a new audience. Your books can be listed at a more competitive price. Your customers get free second day shipping, so you limit the competition in your niche. They get a deal, and you're able to charge more. You can spend more of your time to concentrate on sourcing and listing books, while Amazon's massive distribution system steps up to delivery your products to customers.

Cons -- Little customer service control. Must pay ongoing inventory fees. Extra costs of shipping books must be weighed against entry-level program. If your books don't sell, you have to pay to have them shipped back to you or – worse yet – you have to pay about 50 cents a title to have them disposed of!

Here's how the FBA program works:

http://www.amazonservices.com/content/fulfillment-by-amazon.htm?mkt_tok=3RkMMJWWfF9wsRoluazJZK XonjHpfsX66uwlXaCzgZ9rn0V%2Fe%2BDGNkbLjdV 4GM9gMrDHRxEFEaBzxQpRAr2UcYFa9ftYHg%3D %3D#how-it-works

Features and benefits of using FBA:

http://www.amazonservices.com/content/fulfillment-by-amazon.htm?mkt_tok=3RkMMJWWfF9wsRoluazJZK XonjHpfsX66uwlXaCzgZ9rn0V%2Fe%2BDGNkbLjdV 4GM9gMrDHRxEFEaBzxQpRAr2UcYFa9ftYHg%3D %3D#features-and-benefits

Costs and pricing of the FBA program:

http://www.amazonservices.com/content/fulfillment-by-

To better explain the advantages of the FBA program, I asked Rob Anderson at DollarMoves.com to help answer some common questions people have about FBA:

Rob, tell me what is the best way for the average person to get started with FBA? Describe the best start-up scenario:

I started out with FBA so I only know selling on Amazon via the FBA platform. I started out by purchasing a course that taught me how to sell on Amazon's FBA platform.

I believe that people that are already selling on Amazon via Merchant Fulfilled can just change their current listings to FBA and send their product in. Amazon makes starting FBA really easy!

In your opinion, what are the biggest challenges facing new booksellers with FBA? What are the biggest opportunities?

I think the biggest thing that some people may perceive as a "challenge" is the idea of "letting go" of their product. Not having control of one's product can really mess with people's heads. I have seen many booksellers that were selling on Amazon "Merchant Fulfilled" that switched to FBA and were very nervous…then a few weeks later they couldn't believe they waited so long!

How did you get started selling in the FBA program? Can you share your story with readers on how you got started?

I have another business that deals with the RV industry. When the recession hit the business slowed down quite a bit. In March of 2010 during a semi-failed business trip where my business partner and I traveled from Oregon to Southern California I decided I had to figure something else out (I have a video of this story here: http://www.youtube.com/watch?v=M4TooNvHLV8) and started looking online for ideas about selling on Amazon.

I had thought about selling online before but with all of the business travel that we had been doing to keep the business going I couldn't figure out how (or if I even could) "close" my store to work the business around the traveling.

I somehow came across Nathan Holmquist's e-book that introduced me to FBA. I had not even heard of it before that…I always bought from people that sold FBA so that I could get the free shipping on orders $25 (but I didn't know they were FBA)…I just like free shipping! His book introduced me to the Proven Amazon Course and from there I started my FBA business!

(You can learn more about Rob's recommended resources at his very helpful website: http://www.DollarMoves.com)

What do you wish you knew then that you know now?

If you send in higher priced books you make money so much faster. I used to sell books at ranges as low as $6 each but now I hardly ever sell a book for $10. I TRY and sell books in the $25 range as that gets the free shipping for everyone and also it's much nicer to have the higher margins. I don't like working for a dollar or two per sale.

What shortcuts have you learned that you would recommend to new sellers trying to get traction with FBA?

1. Use a PDA scanner while scouting books for maximum speed…and ALWAYS have a scanner available wherever you are!
2. Shoot to send in a couple boxes a week…the more you send in the more chances you have to make money!
3. Make sure you have good margins on your books BEFORE you send them in (and preferably BEFORE YOU BUY!). With apps and the FBA calculator there is NO NEED TO

EVER GUESS if a book is worthy of sending to FBA.

What would you warn people about when it comes to FBA?

There are extra fees involved so you need to know your numbers. Penny books make no sense when sending books in to Amazon's warehouses. You can send in whatever you want and Amazon will sell it for whatever price you put on it...even if your price means that you lose money!

What is the downside to selling FBA? What is the upside?

I guess a downside would be that if a person has a specific question about a book (I've had two or three people out of thousands ask me specifics about a book) you do not physically have the book in your possession to answer the question. Also there is the return policy but for myself it hasn't been that bad.

There are so many upside's...People will pay more money for a FBA book than for the exact same book Merchant Fulfilled. I have literally sold a book for $35 dollars when the EXACT SAME BOOK IN THE SAME CONDITION was selling for $6! I have done that numerous times with the "magic $25" price point...people are paying for convenience and they trust that Amazon will get their product to them FAST and there is the A to Z return policy that people feel confident in buying directly f

What time frame should people expect to wait before they start making money selling with FBA?

It really depends on what you are sending in to Amazon. If you are sending in product with high demand there are times that my products have sold as soon as the boxes are being processed at the warehouse! Lower ranking books sell quickly while the higher "long tail" books can take a long time... but you never know. I have sold 1 million+ rank books as soon as they get to the warehouse also (although that is not normal).

Please share how much inventory and supplies someone needs to be successful in the FBA program:

As I said previously as far as inventory is concerned the more you have at the warehouses the more chances that you have to sell. I would recommend sending in as much high quality desirable inventory as you can! People's sales tend to double and triple when they start selling via FBA (this is what I have heard from book sellers that start using FBA to sell).

As far as supplies I would recommend having some type of scanning apparatus (either a smart phone an app OR a PDA with database software). Using a laser scanner is much faster than just using the camera on your phone…and using a PDA is the fastest of all and does not require any type of "cell" signal.

You'll also want boxes, tape, tape gun, Dymo printer (if using a listing service like ScanPower), scale, computer, printer, I like having a corded laser scanner to input my books via barcode, void fill…a lot of the things that you would have if doing Merchant Fulfilled.

What books or resources do you recommend to help the new bookseller get up and running on FBA, or where to turn if their business is not making them money?

The Proven Amazon Course helped me out quite a bit. I would really recommend selling more than just books to have more options for customers to buy. With FBA you can just about sell anything with a barcode. I like having many different types of products for sale to insure that I am constantly selling even if my book sales are slow.

If someone wanted to start FBA from scratch with a heavy slant toward selling books I would recommend Cynthia Stine's book "Make Thousands on Amazon in 10 Hours a Week" (here is a video review I did of that book: http://www.youtube.com/watch?v=wa2O-MZoPwc). She talks a lot about selling books and media on Amazon via the FBA platform and she also shows step-by-step screen shots of what to do when setting up an Amazon FBA business.

Do you have alternate ways people can make money selling books online? (EBay.com, Half.com, Craislist.org, or other outlets?)

I personally only sell on Amazon via FBA. I have heard of the other places but have not found a need (currently) to try selling on other venues. With FBA you can sell via different platforms and have Amazon send your product to your customer and Amazon will charge you for it...but again that is something that I have not looked into doing yet.

What is your outlook for the future of selling used books online?

I think that there are always going to be books that are being sold online that are non-fiction very specific type of books. I also think there are a lot of people that just like having a good book to read (the real kind). I have a Kindle Fire HD and I completely prefer reading real books. I think that Amazon keeps growing and so do the customers that are checking it out every day.

People are now looking at Amazon as the first place before they make purchases and I think that trend will continue to happen. As I said the other day to someone...my kids do not remember a world without Amazon (17 and 13 years old)! I can't see the future but I tend to think that the "type" of books that we specialize in are going to continue to sell for a while but I would caution that with electronic book readers there may be a time in the future when most people prefer reading digital copies of books. I think we need to take advantage of the opportunity that we have now while it is still a viable business!

Rob's insight demonstrates that FBA does indeed offer a unique opportunity to sell used books online without the need to ship your own used books, CDs or college textbooks. Utilizing FBA allows you to warehouse your items with Amazon, and the shipments go out direct from Amazon.

To learn more about Rob's success, visit "FBA Tips" by clicking here: http://www.findhow2.com/fba-tips

I highly recommend it!

All in all, utilizing the Amazon FBA channels for selling products online really comes down to understanding your own needs, goals, time commitment as to whether or not the Amazon FBA program is right for you.

In any event, now it's the time to decide which types of books and related products to stock up on to sell! And that's what the next section will cover.

CHAPTER 10: Stocking Up On The Right Kinds Of Books – Where To Buy 'Em, How To List 'Em, How To Store 'Em 'Til They Sell!

Now that you are signed up as a seller, and you've got bookshelves ready to fill, envelopes ready to stuff and tape guns in your holster ready to do their dirty work, it's time to stock up on books to sell. Buying right will help you make more money. So read and heed!

I'll admit: I got lucky. I found stashes of good-selling books right from the beginning. Having a load of books that I could quickly list and sell to get the money flowing in helped keep my spirits up in the early days of my bookselling venture. But you can do it too. Even if you're only finding 5, 10, 20 books at a time, keep at it and you'll eventually have hundreds of little dirty books making you steady cash.

Online booksellers report that it's not uncommon to pay $1 for a book, then discover once they log onto their account that it's so rare sought after that it brings in $50, $75, maybe $100 or more, simply because it was signed by the author or it was a First Edition, or it was a limited short run book that history buffs are angling to get their hands on.

I remember one big box of books I purchased at an auction had a book by master motivator Zig Zigler, and on the title page he had signed it. Now, I've yet to put that one up for sale, I really like Zigler. But one day maybe I will, and I'm sure having his signature on it, and the condition being as good as it is, that book ought to bring me a tidy profit!

You should avoid certain types of books that will only take up space in your home and usually won't sell well anyway. If you do get stuck with them when you buy a large lot of books at garage sales, estate sales or auctions, there is a way to profit on these: donate them to local non-profit thrift stores in your area for a tax deduction off your taxes.

Fiction doesn't sell well for me. Now, if you have found a rare Ernest Hemmingway First Edition hardcover, you've found a gem. But most times I'm convinced that fiction buyers would rather buy their book direct from a bookstore or from the publisher direct.

Also, my experience with books put out by Readers Digest or Rodale Press has been less than stellar. I don't know why; they are good books, good information, written and illustrated to help people solve common, everyday problems like weight loss, health, home repair. My suspicion is that these publishers use their magazines and direct mail marketing prowess to flood the market with so many of these books that the people who DO want to buy them already have them. Buyers scouring Amazon are looking for that "something different" and you've got to be able to deliver.

Some used library books sell OK. You've got to make sure you add to your listing that the book is an ex-library book. Those types of books will be pretty good because they usually don't have a lot of margin scribbling or highlighting in them -- however, they DO have regular library markings and if they are pretty old, they will have library card pockets. In some cases, I've found and resold ex-library books that have a big, obnoxious "Discarded" or "Withdrawn" rubber stamp right on the front cover. This doesn't come off. Just make sure you mention it in your listing. If the buyer wants the book bad enough, they won't mind the stamp on the cover.

Bestselling books that are always in high demand at Amazon

Never pass these dirty little books up and you'll always be in the money:

UFOs & Aliens (always a good seller!)

Astrology

New Age

Celebrity Biographies (especially vintage copies)

Teacher Classroom Resource Guides

History (Especially European history books with photos)

Conspiracy theory books

Language books

Self-help How-to books

Like I said before, you'll find these little gems at garage sales, at estate auctions, at thrift stores, and at library fundraising 'book sales' all the time. The secret is to focus in on the ones that are in high demand, are in the best condition you can find (or can be cleaned up for a quick sale), and are selling for 50 cents apiece, or less.

(Tip: At garage sales and some thrift stores, I've offered a lower price by offering to pay a flat amount.... Lower amount than if I'd bought them separately .... If I take a whole box off their hands. I know I'll be taking home some clunkers, but even after taking those out of the mix, I often can get the books for 10 cents each or less. I've often recouped my investment with the sale of just one of the books, and the rest are free and clear! I can price them low for quick sale, or even put them into a yard sale of my own in the future for 25 cents apiece!)

Don't be afraid to ask for a discount... all they can say is 'No.'

Pricing Your Books For Top Profits, Quick Sales

If you can type in a 10 digit number and use an Internet browser scrollbar, then you can spy on what others are selling your book for, and you can price accordingly. I'll share my own pricing strategies for different kinds of hot sellers.

I usually set prices of the books I list on Amazon competitive with the current used prices offered by other LIKE booksellers.

What do I mean by this? I mean to say that I don't always list the lowest price offered. Instead, because I have cultivated a 5-Star 100% Satisfied Rating, I look for sellers who have a 97% or better rating and check their pricing on the same book.

I often disregard the pricing of sellers offering 1 cent books. I have no idea why they sell themselves short. Many speculate that they do so much volume that they make up for the insanely cheaper price by moving tons of books through the post office. Or, perhaps they never ship the books. Who knows. I focus on books people want and I sell them at a reasonable price, and offer prompt, guaranteed delivery. If the book is not what I promised or described, they can send it back and I'll pay for the shipping both ways. Over the long term I feel that's the best way to stay in the money.

I believe you'll make more money by pricing just a little above the lowest price, but not too high that you'll be babysitting your inventory for more than 6 months.

Here's a recent snapshot of sales activity in my account, showing selling prices and competitor prices. You can see that often I'm the low price… but not always!

The Night Battles: Witchcraft & Agrarian Cults in the Sixteenth & Seventeenth...	01/12/2012 13:34:26	0	Used - Good	$7.99	$ 6.24	Inactive (Out of Stock)
The Story of Edgar Cayce [Unknown Binding]	01/07/2012 13:52:32	0	Used - Good	$9.99		Inactive (Out of Stock)
World Without Cancer: The Story of Vitamin B 17 by Griffin, G. Edward	01/07/2012 13:08:03	0	Used - Good	$8.99		Inactive (Out of Stock)
Fight the Good Fight [Perfect Paperback] by Dr. Mac McCrory	01/06/2012 21:07:33	0	Used - Very Good	$6.39		Inactive (Out of Stock)
Silence, Solitude, Simplicity: A Hermit's Love Affair with a Noisy, Crowded, ...	01/06/2012 15:13:49	0	Used - Like New	$7.50		Inactive (Out of Stock)
Coaching People to Train Their Dogs by Terry Ryan	01/06/2012 06:25:42	0	Used - Very Good	$19.99		Inactive (Out of Stock)
Hot Commodities: How Anyone Can Invest Profitably in the World's Best Market	01/05/2012 18:11:28	0	Used - Like New	$7.98	$ 6.79	Inactive (Out of Stock)
Teaching Grammar in Context [Paperback] by Weaver, Constance	01/04/2012 14:09:03	0	Used - Good	$6.99		Inactive (Out of Stock)
The Cathars & Reincarnation by Guirdham M.D., Arthur	01/03/2012 17:01:20	0	Used - Very Good	$8.99	$ 3.27	Inactive (Out of Stock)
Holy Cows And Hog Heaven: The Food Buyer's Guide To Farm Friendly Food	01/03/2012 09:06:55	0	Used - Very Good	$6.50	$ 3.00	Inactive (Out of Stock)
Ordeal Book 1 the Sisters [Hardcover] by Alexei Tolstoy	01/01/2012 05:24:14	0	Used - Very Good	$12.50		Inactive (Out of Stock)
Wars of the Roses by Ross, Charles	12/29/2011 21:57:31	0	Used - Very Good	$6.99		Inactive (Out of Stock)
Folk Songs of Trinidad and Tobago, Collected and edited with additional mater...	12/29/2011 14:32:03	0	Used - Good	$21.99		Inactive (Out of Stock)
Secret Prophecy of Fatima Revealed: New Age Visions of the Virgin Mary	12/29/2011 06:37:43	0	New	$8.75		Inactive (Out of Stock)

You've got to be able to turn the book inventory you've got, unless it's yours free and clear. Then, you can afford to sit on the inventory, provided you have the space and you'll not squeezed to find room for new treasures you'll be finding every month.

As an example, let's use the book on my bookshelf next to my desk: "Alternative Cures" by Bill Gottlief. I usually type in the 10-digit ISBN number – found either on inside title page or on the back cover, usually right above the UPC code – to get the current pricing on the book. But you can also just type in the title of the book. I type in "Alternative Cures" in the Find It on Amazon search box. Here's a screenshot of the results:

This screen shows the various books available. The copy I have is the third one down from the top. Clicking on the hyperlink "See all product details" takes me to the description page, showing lowest prices for new and used titles. To the right, notice the yellow "Sell yours" button; by clicking on that, I get a screen like the one below, displaying the seller listing form:

In drop down box I select the correct condition of the book, and then copy-and-paste the pre-written condition note into the box below that. If there is something unusual about this book – maybe it's signed by author, or it's a first edition, or there is highlighting throughout the text of the book – I note those differences. Then I type in the price and quantity (Here I only have one; once in a while you'll list more than one of the same item, but not often though), and scroll down to bottom and click Submit. Review and submit again. Within minutes, this book is on sale on Amazon!

And here is the email I receive instantly:

Dear JPC Books & More,

Thank you for listing your product at Amazon.com. Your listing will be available for purchase on our site within minutes. However, it may take up to 15 minutes for the listing to appear in the open listings area of your seller account. Please do not re-list the product if you do not see the open listing immediately. Your listing will remain open until it is purchased.

Here are the details of your listing:

Title: Alternative Cures (Alternative Cures: The Most Effective Natural Home Remedies for 160 Health Problems (Hardcover))
Quantity remaining: 1
Total quantity sold: 0
Buyer's price: $9.99
Amazon commission (if sold): (Standard Shipping)
Standard Shipping credit (if sold): $3.99
Condition: Used - Good
Comments: Good condition. Hardcover. No markings inside pages. Cover and binding good. In stock ready to ship. We ship USPS standard media mail.

Listing ID: 0126MOR58L6
SKU: SK-Y4DU-FNI4

When your listing appears in your seller account, you will see it linked to the corresponding detail page in the Amazon.com catalog: http://www.amazon.com/gp/offer-listing/B000S6IDQO

Amazon.com will contact you by e-mail as soon as a buyer places an order for your item(s). However, since email is not always a reliable form of communication, we recommend that you also access your seller account at least once a day to check for new orders.

As you can see in the screenshot above, the book I listed (it's right in the middle) winds up getting ranked by price, so my book is not found until the buyer scrolls through to the third page of results. This is unlikely to happen, and at this point, I'm very doubtful the book will sell unless I go back into the *Manage Inventory* screen and lower the price by half.... And then I wouldn't make a dime of the book after postage and seller fees! Best to leave it be for now.... And maybe read the book for enjoyment or some education on natural health cures!

I can usually list an average of 20 to 30 books an hour using the basic online 'Add An Item' form, then I need to take a break, and hit it again after about 10-15 minutes away from the laptop. So, in 2 hours, I can list 40-60 books. Do this every day and within a month you can add between 1,200 to 1,500 books, DVDs, CDs or whatever you're selling to your seller account inventory.

Once you list them, store your books on your bookshelves in an easy-to-remember method that will allow you to locate and retrieve your books quickly when they finally do sell. Group books by category, or alphabetically, or by any system that works for YOU.

Take it from me: it is FRUSTRATING to spend 20 minutes looking for a book that sold for less than $6 or $7 – a book you're only going to earn $3 at best – because you forgot which bookshelf you placed it on!

You probably will be able to beat me in the time it takes you to list books. But here's how I do it:

Step-by-step listing process

 I don't type really fast, and I take some time to look over the book I'm adding to my online inventory to make sure I describe it accurately. The reason it takes me 2 minutes to list most of the books I find is that I need to:

1. Type in the ISBN number (This is the 10 or 13 digit number usually printed on the back cover, or on the inside publisher's title page)

2. Click on the USED BOOK pricing tab

3. Drill down into the listings. The cheapest books will rise to the stop. Some will be the 'Fulfilled By Amazon' books that are selling for 1 cent plus $3.99 shipping and handling. Scroll down lower. If you start seeing $6.99, $9.99, $11.99 pricing within the first 10 listings, go ahead and list yours too. If you reach the second or third page and the books are still selling for $1 or $2, set that book aside and check the pricing on the next book in your lot. It may not be worth your time to list that book after all.

4. If pricing is lucrative enough to post for sell, I'll click on "Sell Yours Here" tab. If not, then I make a decision on whether to pitch the book or set it aside in the YARD SALE bin. (Tip: These books still have some value. I'll show you later on how you can get a tax deduction by donating these books to a non-profit

that runs a thrift store in your hometown, and potentially lowering your tax bill!)

5. Listing form appears. List the condition (have the book handy to describe the condition of the cover, the spine, the binding, any writing or highlighting on inside text pages, any rips or tears or stains or stickers on the book itself). I use a copy-and-paste procedure (see examples below) that helps cut this down to 30 seconds after a little bit of practice.

6. Price your book. If you're unsure, price it at 20 times what you paid for it. If you paid 50 cents, list it for $9.99. You can edit it later. There is a feature where you can match the lowest price. I don't use this. There are lots of software programs that allow sellers to raise and lower and raise back up their pricing in seconds, and I'd hate to get my books caught up in that up and down frenzy, and wind up selling a book for less than I want it to.

7. Click on SUBMIT button.

8. On the next screen you'll double check your description. Take 15 seconds to scan through it. If you missed something or have a typo, now's the time to fix it. Click the EDIT button, make your corrections, and submit again.

9. Click on final SUBMIT button and buyers will be able to buy your book within a matter of minutes. I

usually see the new book listed in my INVENTORY screen within 30 seconds. There's really no need to wait to see it though. Set the book aside. Grab the next. Repeat the above process for 30 books. Then take a break. Go get a cup of coffee or a soda. This is a good time to double check your inventory screen, scanning through titles to make sure you didn't list an Acceptable quality book as a "Like New" book, or that you mispriced a book. This is also the time to check the competing prices; if it is just a few pennies cheaper, I go ahead and re-price mine 5-25 cents cheaper, and try to get the quick sale just in case somebody is searching for that title right that minute.

Your next step: take those 30 books and arrange them on your shelving in one place. You'll need to come up with your own filing system to retrieve sold books quickly and without a major scavenger hunt in your home. By placing them all in one place you'll find most times you will remember what the book looked like (if you forget, click on the listing link and refer to the photo of the book), seek it out, and set it aside for mailing.

I usually only ship books every other day. You have 2 days to ship the books. I like to limit my wait time in U.S. Post Office lines. I have a shelf in my home office where I place the books that have sold. If I have 5-6 books that sell in one day, and I have the time, I'll make an exception to this rule and I'll package them up, address them, tape them up for shipping, and deliver them to the post office. But only if it doesn't put me off track with the plans I've already made that day for my business.

I have never had a problem waiting the 2 days to accumulate enough orders to make the trip downtown to the post office and make the trip worthwhile for me. I figure most buyers realize that when they have selected the standard shipping service (the cheapest option) that they are willing to wait for the book. Otherwise, they would have selected the 2-Day or Overnight options, or they would belong to the Amazon Prime program, where they get free 2-day shipping with all book orders.

Next, I'll share with you my tips on writing better descriptions to help you sell more used books faster.

CHAPTER 11: Writing Accurate Descriptions When Listing Your Books, CDs & DVDs For Sale

Probably the most important thing you will have control over when you list your book is to add a full, sell-able description of your book in the listing form.

- Put in what the buyer wants to know.
- Put in what the buyer needs to know.
- Put in what the buyer might be surprised to know.
- Put in a secondary reason to buy.
- Tell the buyer he or she can be confident that the book will be packed well and shipped promptly.
- Offer a freebie (i.e., free delivery confirmation)

Here are some samples I've used that seem to work very well. I have these on a template page loaded onto my computer. I pull up the listings (they are in very basic Notepad text format to avoid having data conversion problems if they were in MS Office or some-such other word processing software program which seems compelled to add strange formatting options to what I type), and all I have to do is copy-and-paste the description which closely matches what I'm selling, insert it into the right spot on the form, then go in and edit it 10-15 seconds to accurately match the book's condition.

Example Listing:

Condition: Used - Good

Comments: Good condition, hardcover, sixth printing 1952. No dust cover. Except for 2 inscriptions inside front cover, there is no writing or highlighting noted on the inside pages. Edges and spine of cover scuffed lightly, spine OK, binding OK. Good copy for reading or research on this topic. In stock and ready to ship today. We ship USPS standard media mail with free delivery confirmation to ensure timely, accurate delivery direct to you.

Lately I've been adding in the fact that my own seller rating is quite high. I start off the listing this way:

"Buy with confidence from 5-Star Amazon Marketplace Seller!"

This type of comment aims to build confidence; I want to bring their attention to that, and to set their mind at ease so they won't wonder if they are risking their money buying my book over the other 50 books of the same title bidding for their attention. Many sellers mention their turnaround times ("We ship same day!") or number of books shipped per day ("Thousands shipped daily!") or some other promise of dependability.

Example of how to copy and paste:

I've found it's much easier to type up the description of books in Notepad, then copy and paste using old-school keyboard techniques. To do this, use your mouse or your laptop mouse to highlight the text your want to copy, then hold down the CTRL button at the bottom left of your computer keyboard and press the "C" key. That copies it.

Go over to the screen showing your Amazon book listing form, click your cursor onto the "Comments" box, the hold down the CTRL button and press the "V" key. This pastes it into the form. Saves you tons of typing. If I need to make a small change to the copy – say, for instance, the spine on a paperback is creased and torn slightly – then I can scroll to that part of the description, type it in, and click the "Submit" button. All done!

Move on to the next book.

Copy. Rinse. Repeat.

Nothing could be easier!

Importance of accurately and fully describing your book when listing on Amazon

Describing the condition of your book is so important to your success as an Amazon Seller that I've included Amazon's own words on the subject below.

(To check for latest updates or changes to their policies, visit: http://www.amazon.com/gp/help/customer/display.html?nodeId=1161242)

Books

Guidelines for New and Used Books items:

- *New*: Just like it sounds. A brand-new, unused, unread copy in perfect condition.
- *Like New*: An apparently unread copy in perfect condition. Dust cover is intact, with no nicks or tears. Spine has no signs of creasing. Pages are clean and are not marred by notes or folds of any kind. Book may contain a remainder mark on an outside edge but this should be noted in listing comments.
- *Very Good*: A copy that has been read, but remains in excellent condition. Pages are intact and are not marred by notes or highlighting. The spine remains undamaged.
- *Good*: A copy that has been read, but remains in clean condition. All pages are intact, and the cover is intact (including dust cover, if applicable). The spine may show signs of wear. Pages can include limited notes and highlighting, and the copy can include "From the library of" labels.
- *Acceptable*: A readable copy. All pages are intact, and the cover is intact (the dust cover may be missing). Pages can include

considerable notes--in pen or highlighter--but the notes cannot obscure the text.

- *Unacceptable*: Moldy, badly stained, or unclean copies are not acceptable, nor are copies with missing pages or obscured text. Books that are distributed for promotional use only are prohibited. This includes advance reading copies (ARCs) and uncorrected proof copies.

Take your time to describe your books in an accurate manner. An accurate product description increases buyer satisfaction, helps sellers build a loyal customer base, and ensures positive feedback ratings. Should a book have an obvious cosmetic flaw, sellers must make a note within the comments field. The presence of a remainder mark should always be noted in comments. Advance reading copies and uncorrected proofs are not permitted.

As a rule of thumb, only list Used – Good, Used – Very Good, and Used – Like New book conditions. It's not a bad idea when started out – at least until you understand the rating system for describing books – that you UNDER-rate your book. That means, if you consider it Used – Like New, go ahead and drop down one more ranking, and list it as Used – Very Good. Then, within the description go ahead and add your own comment that the book looks like it was never read, looks new, etc.

CHAPTER 12: Is There Money To Be Made In The College Textbook Market Anymore?

Probably the worst financial decision you can make in college -- besides taking out way too many college loans that is – would be keeping your college classroom textbooks and thinking they would have some value in your future career. They won't. Sell them for whatever they will fetch now. Amazon allows you to do that yourself. And, if you want to locate, list, and sell textbooks, it's easier than ever to do that online these days.

Sellers do profit from used text books that students have to buy for college classes. Pick them up for pennies, sell for big bucks. But there are dangers to look out for. You don't want to get stuck with unsellable or outdated books, and you don't want all your profits eaten up with shipping costs, either. Most textbooks are heavy. They cost a lot to mail. Just keep that in mind when you're buying or listing them. I'd recommend only selling textbooks that you get for free or for little of nothing to experiment before jumping in as a full-time textbook seller.

In January 2012, Apple announces new partnerships that will bring digital textbooks to students — a $10 billion industry that rarely embraces changes sweeping other industries.

(Read the link below to learn more about how the school textbook industry could change)

http://www.washingtonpost.com/business/technology/apple-expected-to-delve-into-textbooks/2012/01/18/gIQA52iH9P_story.html?tid=pm_business_pop

(And here's another story on the roll-out announcement)

http://gadgetbox.msnbc.msn.com/_news/2012/01/19/10188912-apple-to-announce-new-digital-textbook-service

CNET.com weighed in with overview article that asks the questions, "6 Things We Don't Know About Apple's E-Textbooks Strategy"

http://reviews.cnet.com/8301-31747_7-57361974-243/6-things-we-dont-know-about-apples-e-textbooks-strategy/

My own experience is that textbooks can make good extra profits, but the ones I've found in 'Very Good' and 'Like New' condition are rare.

But sometimes I do get lucky. Here is a picture of one textbook I bought for 50 cents at a yard sale on a Saturday morning, listed on the Amazon Marketplace when I got back home that afternoon, and sold it that same evening for $24.95:

I've limited buying textbooks to only those which have zero highlighting or note taking in the margins. I look for clean inside text pages, and I like good looking covers but will accept a few creases or markings on front or back covers. If there was a CD-ROM included in the textbook and it's now missing, I tend to leave those behind. I have indeed bought and sold those, noting in the listing that the CD was missing, but I generally don't make much profit on those.

Finally, my experience is that textbooks take up quite a lot of space in my inventory bookshelves while moving rather slowly overall. Of course, because these items tend to sell well just 2-3 times a year along with college semesters, I'll see spikes in textbooks just a few weeks out of the year.

Next: How to sell multiple books at one time.

CHAPTER 13: Make Money Selling Book Lots On EBay

If you're having trouble moving books in a certain niche, selling a bundle of books on EBay may be a benefit. You'll need to set-up your own EBay account and learn how to list (it's fairly simple to learn). You'll need a PayPal account to collect your money. Below, you'll see a couple recent book lots I sold in EBay auctions. I'd recommend bundling at least 6 books in the lot and keeping the titles all in the same niche subject.

Here's a picture of one book lot that sold:

This is a book lot containing 6 books (1 hardcover, 5 paperback) which I listed and sold recently on EBay for $36.07.

I was going to add "Barnes Bullets Reloading Manual" (pictured below) to "sweeten the offer" but when I was ready to list the book lot, I changed my mind and kept it listed for sale in my Amazon Marketplace listings. That single book sold 3 days after I posted the book lot on EBay, and it sold for $14.00, giving me a nice profit; I had purchased it at a local thrift store for only $1 about 2 months previously.

I think I made the right decision. I doubt adding this one book to the six piece book lot would have increased the Ebay auction revenue. I'd have lost money.

Lesson learned: Be careful with book lots. Don't give too much away. If you have a title which is in a niche category and it's relatively selling well, keep it out of your book lot sales on EBay.

Another lesson: Owing to the recent news regarding gun control and the fact ammunition is getting harder to find, it seems to me very reasonable that this book became more popular as gun owners turned to 'how-to' books to learn ways they could make their own ammo.

Here is another book lot I sold recently:

It was a collection of martial arts books that was part of a large lot purchase I bought in the summer of 2012. Most of the books sold for $10 to $50+ over that time listed on Amazon Marketplace.

This book lot sold for $12.99. Fortunately, the same buyer bought both book lots at the same time, with shipment for both book lots to the same address. The total sale was over $49.00, and my net profit after paying for the cost of the books, my EBay fees, my PayPal final value fees, and USPS shipping was right at $30.00. In the end I felt good about this sale: I moved books I needed to clear out of inventory, and I made a decent profit.

Bottomline, book lots can help you move a large number of books at one time to clean out slow-moving inventory. But the downside is that you'll likely spend more time listing them, packing them and shipping them than you'd like, for less money per book than you're regular Amazon Marketplace sales.

Next: How to run your home-based bookstore operations to ensure you get great customer feedback, which will help you sell more used books over the long haul.

CHAPTER 14: How to Get Positive Feedback From Orders You Fulfill on the Books You Sell

Follow these simple tips and you'll almost always eliminate negative feedback. (Of course you can't please everyone, so we tell you what to do when you DO get negative feedback. Relax it's not the end of the world!)

- Ship books when promised.
- Pack carefully to avoid damage to books.
- Confirm promptly.
- Message buyer if there is going to be a delay, or if the product is not available any longer.

Here's a copy of my recent feedback in my Amazon Seller Account (cropped to remove the buyers' names and order numbers) which shows how nice – and profitable – it is to get excellent feedback.

Feedback 1

https://sellercentral.amazon.com/gp/feedback-manager/home.html/ref=m_feedback_cont_home

ogle AdSense – ...   Google   Infolinks   Yahoo! Mail: The be...   Kindle Direct Publis...   ABA Content - Welc.

Rating	Comments	Arrived on Time	Item as Described
5	Item quality, delivery time, and service were excellent. RESPOND	Yes	Yes
5	Very good experience. Book arrived as described. In fact better than described. RESPOND	Yes	Yes
5	Product as described, fast delivery. RESPOND	Yes	Yes
5	Quick shipping. Thank you! RESPOND	Yes	Yes
5	Great service! RESPOND	Yes	Yes
5	Great bookseller. RESPOND	Yes	Yes
5	Great service. RESPOND	Yes	Yes
5	Thank you. RESPOND	Yes	Yes
5	Item as described and in good condition. Arrived on time, perfect transaction. Thanks! RESPOND	Yes	Yes

As the feedback above suggests, people are mainly concerned that the item arrived on time and that it was described accurately! Stay true to those two concerns and you'll do fine getting your share of good customer feedback.

I am still surprised that used book sales generate little feedback. I guess people are just happy to get the book, CD, or DVD, and they move on with their life, too busy to hash out the transaction.

You can take steps to encourage them to leave feedback, but I tend to let Amazon take care of asking for feedback from customers (remember, people who buy your used books are Amazon's customers, not yours.)

CHAPTER 15: Other Proven Ways to Make Money With Used Books, Vintage Magazines, Music CDs, DVDs, Instructional Workbooks and More

- Be on lookout for public domain content

- Republish/repurpose public domain content yourself

- Review books

- Research popular hobbies, business ideas, follow trends

You can often start your own money-making blog or website commenting on the books that you find. I've found lots of how-to books that bring mere pennies online… but they have helped me research a popular topic on my website, www.FindHow2.com and a host of online blogs I maintain.

I'm not advocating copyright infringement here. I'm talking about having a ready-made resource of how-to information, kind of like a checklist of info that will help you write on popular and profitable subject with authority, and help people find help on what they are searching for. In the instance of FindHow2.com, we target a problem people are having – for instance, one popular subject that gets lots of internet search traffic is how to pay off your student loans – and the outdated books on the topic gave me a ton of pre-researched information to get started looking. I found that many of the websites those books recommended were inactive; but I found the replacement, or I found a better website to recommend.

I found free articles offered by content providers and websites like EzineArticles.com offers republishing options for free when you use a limited number of their author articles that they've assembled to cover practically every subject under the sun. Having your own website means that you can find new ways to monetize this content. I make money by giving away free information. If you want to learn how I do it, check out this free guide at http://www.findhow2.com/httprofits/index.htm

I got started free at www.Blogger.com – I had read an online newspaper summary of their top 20 most popular posts during the month, and I noticed that many of the how-to articles people were emailing to their friends or commenting on centered around credit card debt, dealing with collection agencies, dealing with student loan debt.... Debt, debt, debt.

So I started a free blog called "How To Fix Your Credit Report" back in 2005, and posted my thoughts, research I'd done, links I found, until March 2006, when I launched www.FindHow2.com

I had been inspired by the stories I read in business magazines and online, about the people who were making money re-purposing how-to information, but I didn't want to be updating short posts on a blog several times a day, struggling to build a steady audience with my already way-too-busy schedule.

So, I opted instead to build what I'd term an "evergreen" website that researches a topic people are already searching for, gives a ton of free information they can use right away, plus lots of links to free helpful sites to continue solving their problems. Sprinkled through the free information is the advertising that helps pay for the website and return me money for my time. Optimizing those web pages to attract free organic search engine traffic and working to pin down link swaps with similar website owners helped to slowly build relevant traffic, and create a new stream of revenue that continues month after month, long after I finished researching, writing and publishing those articles!

On some of the pages that have been active for 5+ years, I earn a small, steady income of revenue -- $1 per day, sometimes over $20 per day – with no effort on my part except to occasionally check content to ensure it's still relevant and update outbound links and edit information as needed. As an example, if an article states that I got the information from a survey that ran in 2010, and it's now 2012, I look for an updated survey result. Or I re-word the paragraph to call it a "recent survey." That keeps the tone of the copy fresh.

So, to get practice on how this works, go ahead and set up your own free blog at Blogger.com, to get the feel and learn how to do it. Learn more at:

http://www.findhow2.com/httprofits/index.htm

CHAPTER 16: Using Technology To Find Profitable Books To Resell Online

There are a host of gadgets and online services available now to help you take the guesswork out of book buying, and saving time (and money) when you are sourcing new inventory.

I personally have found a quick and easy way to check pricing with my mobile phone simply by accessing Amazon online with my Droid smartphone. I simply go to their mobile website and type in the ISBN number.

When I scan through the Used Book listings, I can determine if the book is selling for more than $6. If not, I usually pass, unless it's on a subject that interests me, the price is less than 50 cents, and/or the topic may lend itself to researching a new niche website project. It takes me about 45 seconds to type in the name and get current pricing. It doesn't cost me any extra since I have a decent data plan for mobile Internet access. So, I can check about 40-50 books an hour.

Now, the handheld PDA scanners and mobile computers that scan the books quickly may be a real plus for you if you are jumping in full bore into your book-buying venture.

You have to compare for yourself the different plans. Since they may change frequently, we've added links to some of the most popular services. We are not affiliated with any of these, so we offer up these only for your informational purposes. Check them out carefully before signing up for their service. Most appear to offer a trial period, and I'd recommend against signing a long-term contract.

http://www.asellertool.com/ent/index.html

http://www.scoutpal.com/

http://www.bookscoutpro.com/

http://www.neatoscan.com/Details.aspx

Not everyone will be happy to see you coming with a barcode scanner, though.

Here's an exchange found at a Slate.com online forum, with a response from a woman who runs a thrift store which sells lots of books to online book sellers.

One man complained that "barcode scanner people" should not even be able to attend library books sales, "sneaking around trying to scan books."

His final comment: "They regard books as aluminum cans to be recycled, not books to be read or shared" pretty much sums up his opinion of these types of people. I'm pretty sure he would care much for me, in any case.

But one thrift store owner named Jessica Walter came to the defense of the "barcode scanner people"!

Walter said:

"Actually, they help those books continue to be read, and likely shared, by posting them online and therefore giving them a much wider purchasing audience.

It is actually the library that likely recycles the books if they aren't sold at the sale...ask them, they likely donate them to a local thrift store or recycle them for a small profit through a paper recycling fundraising program. And if they donate them to a thrift store ask that store what they do with the books that do not sell after a certain time period.

Online book sellers regard books like any other retailer regards its products...as something to sell and gain them an income. "

To which I add: "Well said, Ms. Walter!"

So decide for yourself if you have skin thick enough to take on people complaining about your book sourcing methods. But then if you've been to a garage sale or estate sale or rummage sale and have witnessed pushy antique dealers rushing around and grabbing everything valuable in sight, you'll know that book buying is not the only rough-and-tumble arena there is!

No matter if you use high-tech, low-tech or no tech to source your used books inventory, I've found a simple formula that will help me purchase books that have a high potential return on investment.

I used my "Rule of 15" to decide a "Buy/No Buy" signal. This means that if the best price I can purchase a book for is $1, then I want to make sure that this book is currently selling for at least $15 on Amazon (in like condition, of course).

So if I find a book for $2 it must be selling for at least $30 on Amazon, otherwise I'm leaving it where it is. This holds true for books selling for 25-50 cents – they must be selling for 15 times what I pay for them, otherwise I leave them alone.

As you progress building your home-based bookstore and gain experience buying and selling used books, you will acquire a good feel for what might make you money simply by sight. You'll see a used book in a thrift store or at a library book sale table, and you'll just somehow "know" that you've got a winner. But I recommend that you double check pricing the way I described above to ensure that you have a large enough profit margin to make your investment in money and time it will take to clean up, list, package and ship that book worth your trouble. After quite a lot of buying and selling of used books on the Amazon Marketplace website, I've made it a personal rule to list items no less than $9.97, and push to the envelope to get the maximum profit I can out of each used book.

Don't forget that you can always – and should always – review your inventory to make sure you haven't priced for used books too low. One trick to see what the next low price of a book similar to yours is to go into your account settings and put all your listings on vacation mode. Then, over that following day, scroll through all the pages of your inventory page, paying keen attention to the lowest sale price next to yours. I'm often shocked to see that I've underpriced a large number of titles in a vain attempt to gain the lead in a mistaken urge to be out in front of the pack of book sellers for a particular title. But that's stupid. Watch what others are paying for this title. Better yet, watch that there may not be any other competition, and you have complete control over pricing and can name the price you want. Yes, some titles may sit on the shelf for months, maybe a year, but when they do sell, you'll make a huge profit that otherwise might have been lost to you.

CONCLUSION: Summing It All Up

Is that the finish line coming up? Wow, we've covered a lot of territory, you've put up with my ramblings on the tips and techniques I use every week to make easy money selling used books online. I believe now is a good time to review the best way to get started. I've put together a new inventory tracker that anyone can print out and use that fits their own unique circumstances.

Download the form here:
http://www.findhow2.com/sell-on-amazon/index.html

Print a copy out and take a pen or pencil and start writing down all of your goals, your interests, your hobbies, and the time you can commit to get started.

If you don't MAKE the time to do this business, you won't do this business. You'll wonder months from now why you never got around to making money like me selling on Amazon. The reason usually is that the reader never put the book down and put on the work boots to go find the books, sit down and list the books, and run to the Post Office to mail off the orders. Like a famous author once said, "Getting started is being half-finished." Start today setting your goals and set aside the time to make easy money this way.

Set financial goals – how much you want to invest to get started, and how much you would like to make – and to be fair with yourself, start with modest goals.

It's no crime to say you want to start with investing $500 in your business and you want to net $200 a month. I think that is a good place to start. If you can only afford $50 to get started, you'll make much less right off the start, but you'll gain the experience to list, sell, buy, and sell more books, DVDs, CDs, booklets, manuals, comic books, video games, software, what have you, and if you find it enjoyable, keep at it, keep learning, read everything you can about the subject and subscribe to newsletters, RSS feeds, set up Google Alerts to inform you of new developments, and don't stop.

I don't recommend that you 'bet the farm' on this business. By that, if you're having trouble making the rent right now, get a part-time job to bring in more income, and do this business on the sly. Sell something you don't need or you don't use anymore, raise $500, and get started this next week.

As you buy and sell more books, you'll gain confidence that you can do this on a larger scale, and perhaps you'll find an interest in a unique niche that you really like and you can source books to fill that niche.

If that is the case, I hope you also take my advice and learn how to develop your own blog and website.

You may want to grow your business into a full-fledged bookstore with a retail storefront, or you may prefer (like me) to keep it virtual and have more free time, no employee headaches, and a flexible schedule. But enjoy the ride. Live the dream. Keep this in mind: "No matter how far you travel there's always someplace else to go."

This journey we've shared over these many pages is just the beginning. I hope we pass again. In the meantime, visit my free blog at http://sellusedbooksonline.blogspot.com for updated how-to articles, tips and techniques for home-based used booksellers, and let me know how you're doing. Give me some honest feedback for future versions of this book. As you've learned in this book, I don't know it all. But I'm open to knowing it all, and that makes the difference. Let me know if I overlooked something that would have made your bookselling start even easier. I do appreciate it.

Now…. Get out there and find those dirty books and make some easy money!

Good luck!

About the Author:

Steve Johnson runs JPC Books & More, and publishes www.FindHow2.com, as well as authoring numerous how-to articles and e-books.

His blog exploring new tips for selling used books online is found at:

http://sellusedbooksonline.blogspot.com

Also, Steve has published a new Kindle Book on the niche topic of buying and selling old magazines:

HOW TO MAKE

EASY CASH

WITH OLD

MAGAZINES

Make Money Finding, Listing & Selling Used and Vintage Magazines In Your Spare Time!

Steve Johnson
Author of
"How To Make Easy Money Selling
Your Old Used Books on Amazon"

"How To Make Easy Cash With Old Magazines"

By Steve Johnson

Announcing a new Kindle Book that helps guide you to expand your bookselling business by including vintage magazines and older magazines (1980's and older) to your "Sourcing List" and gives you the insider's view into how to make money and keep everything organized.

This book helps you save time, save money, helps you know what to buy and what not to buy, helps cut the clutter, and helps you avoid newbie mistakes.

Why is this so lucrative? Many reasons: Old magazine covers make great wall art. Out-of-print magazine articles and fiction is like gold to hobbyists and historians. Vintage magazine ads are prized by collectors of specific periodicals and of certain product lines.

Take a look at the table of contents to see what you get:

Why You Need To Get This Book Now!

Chapter 1: How Old Magazines Can Make You Money

Chapter 2: Picking the Right Kinds of Magazines to Buy & Resell

Chapter 3: Thrift Store Finds – How a friend bought an old stack of magazines for less than $5, then sold them for $10-30 each online!

Best Places to Look For Old Magazines

Chapter 4: Cut Clutter to Reclaim Your Home and Make Extra Cash at the Same Time

Chapter 5: How to Know What Your Old Magazines Are Really Worth and How To Price Them For Max Profits

Chapter 6: How to Grade Old Magazines For Accurate Listings and To Minimize Negative Feedback

Why You Need To Get A Copy of "How To Make Easy Cash With Old Magazines" Today:

If you want to make money buying and selling old, vintage magazines, this book can help you make more money faster, and avoid getting stuck with trash.

Magazine back issues and vintage magazines deliver an aura of nostalgia – and can help you pocket a pretty profit – when you know what to look for whenever you are out and about sourcing product.

How to sell old magazines is only one part of this book. Magazine collectors can use this guide as a resource to value their collection and learn how to get maximum value when they swap with other collectors.

Selling current magazines or magazine back issues can be an easy way to add extra profits for very little work, low investment, and low risk.

Selling magazines is a lucrative way to supplement your income, working only a few hours a week, and never really doing any selling at all. All you need to do is find old copies of Life Magazine to vintage car magazines, post them for free online, ship them as soon as the orders are e-mailed to you, and automatically collect your profits. So simple, yet so profitable! This is the easy way how you can make money in this niche market.

You might already have a stash of old magazines to sell. Perhaps you've inherited old magazines, or you discovered a large box of forgotten magazines in your attic, or you purchased a box full of used magazines at an estate sale. Either way, you can get top dollar by following the advice in this eBook.

But that ain't the only way to make money in this business! If you're like me, you love prowling yard sales and auctions. Along the way you're bound to run across old magazines. Sometimes you get lucky and you'll find a true diamond in the rough. Maybe you find a seller who just wants to get rid of them all and puts a $1 asking price on the whole box. Or you get them for 25-50 cents each.

In any case, there is money to be made. For about the price of a gallon of gas next time you fill up your car or truck, this e-book can be your investment in locating the diamonds in the rough and leaving the dirt behind. Better yet, you'll find some new ideas and tips on many different ways to profit from old magazines.

Don't delay. Order your copy today and get started making easy cash with old magazines!

You can read a free sample using the "Look Inside" feature on the book's sales page simply by going to:

http://www.amazon.com/dp/B00KQUIAOC

You'll get an 80+ page e-book with real page numbers. Get this book and get a head start making easy cash with old magazines today! Thank you and enjoy!

Steve Johnson

Made in the USA
Middletown, DE
18 January 2020